THE LONDON
Ritz
BOOK OF
Afternoon Tea

Tea! Thou soft, thou sober, sage, and venerable liquid, thou female tongue-running, smile-smoothing, heart-opening, wink-tipping cordial, to whose glorious insipidity I owe the happiest moment of my life, let me fall prostrate.

Colley Cibber, *The Lady's Last Stake*, 1708

THE LONDON

Ritz
BOOK OF
Afternoon Tea

The Art and Pleasures of Taking Tea

————HELEN SIMPSON————

ARBOR HOUSE
WILLIAM MORROW
New York

To Richard

Published in the United States of America by
Arbor House Publishing Company and in
Canada by Fitzhenry & Whiteside Ltd., by
arrangement with Ebury Press, London

First impression 1986
Reprinted four times in 1987
Reprinted twice in 1988

Edited by Suzanne Webber
Art Director: Frank Phillips
Designed by Roger Daniels
Illustrated by Dennis and Sheila Curran

Library of Congress Cataloging-in-Publication Data

Simpson, Helen.
 The London Ritz book of afternoon tea.

 1. Afternoon teas. 2. Tea. 3. Cookery, English.
I. Ritz Hotel (London). II. Title.
TX736.S56 1986   641.5′3   86-8013
ISBN 0-87795-823-8

Filmset by Advanced Filmsetters (Glasgow) Ltd
Printed in Great Britain at the University Press, Cambridge

Acknowledgements
The author would like to thank Michael
Duffell, David Miller, Peter Hyde and Michael
Twomey of The Ritz Hotel, London for their
help.

The publishers would like to thank the
following for permission to reprint copyright
material:
Page 28 Reprinted by permission of
Macdonald and Co (Publishers) Ltd from *Food
in England* by Dorothy Hartley
Page 30 Reprinted by permission of Faber and
Faber Ltd from *Recipes from an Old Farmhouse*
by Alison Uttley
Page 41 Reprinted by permission of Chatto &
Windus from *Remembrance of Things Past* by
Marcel Proust, translated by C K Scott
Moncrieff and Terence Kilmartin

As well as giving recipes for sandwiches and
cakes served at The Ritz Hotel, London this
book includes many more ideas for different
varieties of afternoon tea. The hotel does not
serve all the dishes for which recipes are given
here.

Note on flour for those using Cup Measures
All purpose flour can be substituted for cake
flour, although this may not give such fine
results.

Contents

TEA AT THE RITZ 6

THE HISTORY OF TEA DRINKING 12

SANDWICHES AND SAVOURY DISHES 18

WINTER TEAS 26

ENGLISH CAKES 32

FOREIGN CAKES AND WICKED CAKES 40

HIGH TEA 46

SUMMER TEAS 52

A DIRECTORY OF TEAS 58

INDEX
64

Tea at the Ritz

Tea at the Ritz is the last delicious morsel of Edwardian London. The light is kind, the cakes are frivolous and the tempo is calm, confident and leisurely. Takers of tea perch on rose-coloured Louis XVI chairs at marble tables, sipping their steaming cups of Darjeeling or Earl Grey, while the *belle époque* nymphs look on in Olympian disdain.

The Ritz's stage for afternoon tea is the Palm Court, separated from the ground floor's central gallery by Ionic columns. There are no clocks, and, although it is just possible to glimpse the flash of Piccadilly's taxis and buses if you look hard in the direction of the swing doors, a strange sense of taking a holiday from time heightens the pleasure of taking tea here. People look more beautiful than they do in real life, as this is the most flattering light in Europe, falling mild and clear from the Palm Court's frosted glass ceiling and pink-capped chandeliers.

César Ritz always maintained that nothing put people more at their ease in his hotels than the blandishment of tactful lighting. His widow described in her biography of her husband: 'For weeks Ritz was absorbed in lighting problems. And for hours and hours at a time I would sit while he and an electrician tried the effects of various coloured shades on my complexion! A delicate apricot-pink was found to be the most becoming colour.'

Holding sway over this rose-tinted afternoon tea is the famous nymph of the Palm Court fountain, young tritons blowing conch shells above her, while at her feet a tribe of goldfish flick their tails. Anthony Powell described her in *A Dance to the Music of Time*: 'Although stark naked, the nymph looked immensely respectable; less provocative, indeed, than some of the fully dressed young women seated below her.'

Lady Diana Cooper remembers the Ritz as the first hotel where young women were allowed to go alone to tea. Romantic novelist Barbara Cartland has described tea at the Ritz in the years after the First World War as 'a useful institution for the "also-ran" men: one could meet men, without chaperones, for lunch and tea, so you had lunch with men you were keen on, and tea with the rest.'

A few years ago tea at the Ritz reached such dizzy heights of popularity that there would be crowds milling around on the Savonnerie carpet at the steps of the Palm Court, waiting for a table. This could not be allowed, and now it is necessary to reserve tea at the Ritz. Here is one of the few places outside church or royal garden parties where a woman may wear a hat and feel entirely at ease. In fact, those approaching the Palm Court clad in such garments as jeans, shorts or sneakers will be reluctantly but firmly turned away. Suitably dressed tea-bibbers, however, will be greeted by the Palm Court's Master of Ceremonies, Michael Twomey, who has worked at the Ritz for forty years now. 'Tea at the Ritz is not only sandwiches and cakes but an Occasion,' he says. 'Thank goodness there are still places like this for pure enjoyment, even in the modern world.'

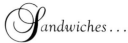

Sandwiches...

Tea at the Ritz, arriving on blue and white china, starts with sandwiches, each crustless finger striped with one of half-a-dozen constant fillings. Down in the Ritz kitchens, it takes the sandwich chef some three hours to provide the afternoon's supply. Extra long loaves are delivered daily, sliced lengthwise in twelve giant strata. Each stratum is spread with softened butter, using a broad spatula knife. Then the fillings are added. Two long slices of brown are placed on top of two long slices of white, and so on, until six great horizontal sandwiches appear in an unbroken wall.

In the brown sandwiches are: thinly sliced cucumber (see page 19); cream cheese beaten with a few chopped chives; smoked salmon with smoked salmon mousse (see page 25). All are lightly seasoned.

In the white sandwiches are: thin slices of smoked ham; egg mayonnaise with mustard and cress (see page 20); finely grated cheddar cheese.

On Sundays, when a Thé Dansant is held in the Ritz's restaurant, there are also sardine-and-mayonnaise sandwiches.

At the end of this procedure with the long loaves, the crusts are shaved from them with a fourteen-inch knife with a serrated blade.

The long bread wall is then sliced at one-inch intervals to produce a multitude of neat stacks of finger sandwiches.

...*Scones*...

Next come scones, plain risen little cakes to eat with cream and jam (see page 55). The Ritz scones are not baked until early afternoon on the day on which they are to be served, to make sure they are as fresh as possible.

...*and Cakes*

Cakes and pastries at a Ritz afternoon tea are airy and Frenchified, extremely pretty, creamy and rich. Crisp shells of *pâte sucrée*, choux and puff pastries are filled with whipped cream and embellished with feather-patterned fondant icing or thin slices of sweet fruit. Head Pastry Chef Peter Hyde and his staff of seven produce a fresh fleet of these cakes every day. Here are recipes for their three most popular pastries.

MILLE FEUILLES

These intricate and exquisite pastries need time, patience and delicate handling in their assembly for perfect results. It is wise to remember that puff pastry can be bought frozen or chilled, and gives excellent results. There is a recipe on page 9 for those who prefer to make their own. Bought fondant can be used if you prefer.

METRIC/IMPERIAL	CUP MEASURES
200 g/7 oz puff pastry ($\frac{1}{2}$ quantity)	$\frac{1}{2}$ quantity (1 sheet frozen) puff pastry
100 g/4 oz seedless raspberry jam	4 tbsp seedless raspberry jelly
300 ml/$\frac{1}{2}$ pint double cream	1$\frac{1}{4}$ cups heavy cream
225 g/8 oz strawberries	$\frac{1}{2}$ lb strawberries
Fondant Icing	Fondant Frosting
1.25 ml/$\frac{1}{4}$ tsp cream of tartar	$\frac{1}{4}$ tsp cream of tartar
300 ml/$\frac{1}{2}$ pint water	1$\frac{1}{4}$ cups water
550 g/1$\frac{1}{4}$ lb granulated sugar	3$\frac{1}{4}$ cups sugar
2–3 drops cochineal	2–3 drops red food colouring
50 g/2 oz plain chocolate, melted	2 squares semi-sweet chocolate, melted

Oven: 450°F/230°C/Mark 8
Makes 6 mille feuilles

Dampen two baking sheets with water. Roll out the puff pastry very thinly into a square of about 30 cm (12 inches). This will be made easier if you roll the pastry between large sheets of greaseproof or wax paper. Cut the pastry into three strips of 10 cm (4 inches) in width. Arrange these strips on the baking sheets, two on one and one on the other. Prick the pastry all over with the prongs of a fork. Chill for half an hour before baking. Bake for 20 minutes until golden.

Allow to cool, then spread two layers of the pastry very thinly with jam. Spread half the cream evenly over one of the pastry strips. Carefully place the other jam-spread strip on top of it, jam side up, and again spread it with cream. Hull and vertically slice the strawberries in three, and bed them down, overlapping, on this coverlet of cream. Gently press the final layer of pastry on top. Tidy escaping cream with a palette knife or spatula. Rest the whole cake in the refrigerator while you make the fondant icing.

Dissolve the cream of tartar in the water over a gentle heat. Pour in the sugar and turn the heat up so that the liquid comes to the boil. It should change from cloudy to translucent. Cover the pan and boil for a few minutes more, until the mixture reaches the soft-ball stage (i.e. when a little of the syrup is dropped into cold water and pressed into a ball, it holds its shape softly). If you have a sugar thermometer, the syrup is ready when it reaches 114°C (238°F). When it has reached this stage, pour it onto a slab of marble or large metal tray and leave for ten minutes or until tepid to touch. Now knead it vigorously with a palette knife or spatula, forming it into a ball then flattening it, repeating this until the syrup whitens, stiffens, and almost crumbles. Set this fondant lump in a heavy pan over a low heat with two or three drops of cochineal or red food colouring. Remove the cake from the refrigerator. Wait for the fondant to soften into a glossy smooth cream, then spread it swiftly over the top surface of the long mille feuilles cake. (Store left-over fondant in a covered glass jar in the refrigerator, it keeps well.) Before the fondant has time to set, pipe very fine lines of the melted chocolate the length of the long cake, about 2.5 cm (1 inch) apart from each other. Draw the back of a small sharp-tipped knife across the width of the mille feuilles at 2 cm ($\frac{3}{4}$ inch) intervals in alternate directions. You will find that this causes the chocolate lines to bend into a linked swallow-wing design of feathery arrows.

Chill the long slice once again in the refrigerator. Now divide this long decorated structure into 5 cm (2 inch) slices using a gentle sawing movement. Chill until ready to serve.

PUFF PASTRY

———METRIC/IMPERIAL———	———CUP MEASURES———
200 g/7 oz strong plain flour	1½ cups unbleached flour
pinch of salt	pinch of salt
200 g/7 oz butter	14 tbsp (1¾ sticks) butter
105 ml/7 tbsp iced water	7 tbsp iced water

Oven: 450°F/230°C/Mark 8
Makes about 400 g/14 oz puff pastry (it is impractical to make smaller amounts so freeze any you do not immediately need)

Sift together the flour and salt. Rub or cut half the butter into the flour, then stir in enough water to make an elastic dough. Knead on a lightly floured surface until smooth, then roll out into a square. Place the remaining butter on one half of the pastry, and enclose it by folding over the other pastry half. Seal the edges by pressing with a rolling pin. Turn the pastry round on the board so the folded edge is to one side, and roll out into a rectangle about three times as long as it is wide. Fold the top third down and the bottom third up and press lightly with a rolling pin. Wrap the pastry in a damp cloth and leave it to 'rest' in the refrigerator for 30 minutes.

Repeat this rolling, folding and resting procedure five times more, each time arranging the newly-folded edge to the side before rolling. After the final resting, roll the pastry into the required shape.

CHOCOLATE ECLAIRS

——METRIC/IMPERIAL—— •	—— CUP MEASURES——
Choux Pastry	*Choux Pastry*
300 ml/½ pint water	1¼ cups water
75 g/3 oz butter	6 tbsp (¾ stick) butter
135 g/5 oz plain flour, sifted	1 cup cake flour, sifted
15 g/½ oz caster sugar	1 tbsp superfine sugar
3 eggs (size 3), beaten	3 large eggs, beaten
Crème Pâtissière	*Crème Pâtissière*
2 eggs (size 3)	2 medium eggs
50 g/2 oz caster sugar	¼ cup sugar
60 ml/4 tbsp plain flour	4 tbsp unbleached flour
300 ml/½ pint milk	1¼ cups milk
50 g/2 oz plain chocolate, melted	2 squares semi-sweet chocolate, melted
300 ml/½ pint double cream	1¼ cups heavy cream
Icing	*Icing*
125 g/4 oz plain chocolate, melted	4 squares semi-sweet chocolate, melted

Oven: 400°F/200°C/Mark 6
Makes 25–30 éclairs

Choux Pastry
Lightly grease two baking sheets. Heat the water and butter to boiling point, then add the sifted flour. Leave over the heat while you stir briskly until the mixture is smooth and leaves the sides of the saucepan. Stir in the sugar. Allow to cool. Beat in the egg, a little at a time. Put the choux pastry (paste) into a piping or pastry bag fitted with a 1 cm (½ inch) star nozzle. Pipe 10 cm (4 inch) lengths onto the baking sheets. Bake for 40 minutes. Turn these hollow puffed-up cigar shapes out on a wire rack; while they are still warm, slit them down one side with a knife so that the steam escapes.

Crème Pâtissière
For the filling, cream together the eggs and sugar. Sift in the flour and stir to a paste with a little of the cold milk. Warm the rest of the milk almost to boiling point, then gradually pour it over the egg mixture, stirring well all the time. Transfer the mixture to a saucepan and stir it over a low heat until it reaches boiling point. Cook for a further five minutes. Remove from the heat and stir in the melted chocolate. Cover and allow to cool. Whip the cream until it is stiff, and keep in a cool place.

For the icing, pour the melted chocolate into a shallow bowl. Take each éclair in turn between finger and thumb with a delicate but firm hold, and dip one side into the warm chocolate. The chocolate sets very quickly.

Now gently prise open each of the éclairs; pipe a narrow line of the chocolate-flavoured *crème pâtissière* along one inside surface and a line of whipped cream along the other. Delicate handling is essential here.

STRAWBERRY TARTS

with a fluted pastry cutter of 8.5 cm (3½ inch) diameter.

METRIC/IMPERIAL	CUP MEASURES
Pâte sucrée	*Pâte sucrée*
100 g/4 oz plain flour	¾ cup unbleached flour
pinch of salt	pinch of salt
50 g/2 oz caster sugar	¼ cup superfine sugar
50 g/2 oz butter	4 tbsp (½ stick) butter
2 egg yolks	2 egg yolks
Filling	*Filling*
1 egg (size 3)	1 medium egg
25 g/1 oz caster sugar	2 tbsp sugar
30 ml/2 tbsp plain flour	2 tbsp unbleached flour
150 ml/¼ pint milk	⅔ cup milk
10 ml/2 tsp kirsch	2 tbsp sugar
150 ml/¼ pint double cream	⅔ cup heavy cream
450 g/1 lb strawberries	1 lb strawberries
60 ml/4 tbsp seedless strawberry jam	4 tbsp seedless strawberry jelly
60 ml/4 tbsp water	¼ cup water
15 g/½ oz desiccated coconut	1 tbsp shredded coconut

Oven: 375°F/190°C/Mark 5
Eight 8.5 cm (3½ inch) shallow patty tins or inverted muffin tins.
Makes 8 tarts

Grease the tins. Sift the flour and salt together onto a working surface. Make a well in the centre and add the sugar, butter and egg yolks. Pinch and work them together, gradually working in all the flour. Add a few drops of water if necessary to bind the mixture together. Knead until smooth, then wrap in foil and leave to 'rest' in the refrigerator for 1 hour. Roll out on a lightly floured surface. Cut out eight circles with a fluted pastry cutter of 8.5 cm (3½ inch) diameter. Arrange these in the patty tins or mould over the inverted muffin tins. Press their inside surfaces with the back of a fork against the sides of each tin hollow. Bake for 20 minutes, until pale gold. Turn out to cool.

For the filling, cream the egg and sugar, sift in the flour and stir to a paste with a few drops of the cold milk. Warm the rest of the milk then stir it in gradually to the egg mixture. Heat the mixture slowly until it reaches boiling point, then cook it for a few more minutes. Remove from the heat, and allow to cool. Stir in the kirsch. Whip the cream until stiff, then beat it into the cooled cream mixture you have just made. Pipe a generous star of the cream mixture into each of the pastry shells. (This two-part cream filling prevents the pastry from becoming soggy, which happens very fast if whipped cream alone is used.)

On each mound of cream plant a whole hulled strawberry, point upwards. Hull and halve the rest of the strawberries. Arrange these halves in a little rampart, slightly overlapping each other, covering the rest of the cream, around the main, whole fruit. If the strawberries are very large, you will probably only need four surrounding halves for each tart. Heat the jam with the water, and use it to paint the strawberry edifices. In your left hand cup a palmful of coconut. With your right hand, deftly turn each tart so that its sticky sides brush against the coconut and become neatly coated.

The History of Tea Drinking

The Chinese, of course, were drinking tea even on the misty borders of recorded time. They kept their pleasure close. The first taste of tea allowed to Europe did not come until the middle of the sixteenth century, when Portugal managed to establish a trading centre at Macao, sending home a few pounds of the precious herb now and then. And once tea reached Europe it was tremendously expensive, the beverage of monarchs and aristocrats alone.

Tay alias Tea

Tea first reached England's shores during the years of Cromwell's Protectorate (1653–1658). The importers tried to make it acceptable to Puritans by selling it as a medicinal draught, advertising it in a London gazette as 'That Excellent and by all Physitians approved *China* drink, called by the *Chineans*

Tcha, by other Nations *Tay alias Tea*.' This did not convince them, however, and it needed the restoration of the Merry Monarch, Charles II, in 1660 to bring tea and pleasure into fashion. Charles married the Portuguese Princess Catherine of Braganza in 1662, and she brought a large chest of tea as part of her dowry. Tea became all the rage at court, taken green, without milk or sugar, from handleless Chinese bowls of blue and white porcelain, hot water poured onto the leaves in oriental style from red-brown stoneware pots.

Soon anybody who was anybody was paying gladly (if dearly) for tea and all its paraphernalia. If you were going in for tea, you had to have a tea service; and if Chinese porcelain or silver were too expensive, this had to be in pewter, faïence or Dutch Delftware, as Europeans had yet to discover how to make porcelain. Then it was necessary to store the valuable tea-leaves in a caddy with compartments for different varieties of tea, a crystal blending bowl and, most importantly, a lock against pilferers. Tea was blended at a little table by the mistress of the house in a pleasingly graceful ritual. Liqueurs like orange-brandy, ratafia and 'Barbadoes-waters' frequently accompanied or followed the tea.

The Democratic Herb

By the eighteenth century tea had become a national passion, and, even though it was so expensive, was brewed throughout the land. Once gentlefolk had drunk the first brew, their servants would make tea for themselves from the used leaves, and then in turn sell the twice-used leaves at the back door. Tea had a great deal to do with improving the national health, too, requiring water to be boiled, and ousting cheap gin (advertised at the time as a good way to get 'Drunk for a penny, dead drunk for twopence'). Rascally tea traders undercut high prices by selling cheap mixtures like smouch, a blend of tea with ash tree leaves boiled in iron sulphate and sheep's dung. Prices were kept outrageously high by various governments, who saw tea as a splendid source of tax revenue. So extortionate was this taxation that no moral twinges were felt by the general public at buying smuggled tea. Clergymen with coastal parishes put their crypts at the disposal of smugglers. Parson Woodforde recorded without shame, 'Andrews the Smuggler brought me this night about 11 o'clock a bagg of Hyson Tea 6 Pd weight. He frightened us a little by whistling

under the Parlour Window just as we were going to bed.' The British government even tried this tea tax on the American Colonies, but the Americans would have none of it. At an enormous fancy-dress tea party in Boston in 1773, where the guests came dressed as Red Indians, they decided to renounce tea in favour of Independence. Pitt the Younger then reduced the tax on tea in 1784, a classic example of locking the door after the horse has bolted.

Tea was taken at breakfast and after dinner, always green and milkless, whether Bohea, Twankey or Hyson. The wealthy poured from oval-bodied or pear-shaped silver teapots into little porcelain cups. Soft-paste porcelain, fine and clear and very expensive, was first made in England in 1745 at Chelsea, decorated with flowers and fables, also appearing as teapots shaped like hens or tulips or artichokes. Competition soon came from Bow (particularly good for oriental scenes in blue and white); from Derby, with magnificent rich colours; and from Worcester, most successful of all with intricate transfer-printed designs and gilding.

Two new London pleasure gardens at Vauxhall and Ranelagh went far in democratising tea. Anyone was allowed in on payment of a small entrance fee, and a noble lady might easily bump into her maid on one of the lantern-lit walks, or over a dish of Bohea. There were suppers, fireworks, mock-Chinese houses, and gallons of tea.

Much of the credit for popularising the habit of tea-drinking, however, must go to one man from Staffordshire, Josiah Wedgwood. He kept his prices low enough to make it possible for all but the poorest to own an elegant tea service (which, as everybody knows, doubles the pleasure of taking tea with friends). A peppery and practical perfectionist, he made sure his wife tried out each new teapot design for pourability, and regularly smashed china at his factory if he saw the slightest flaw. His first tea things were in simple red-brown earthenware, shiny salt-glazed stoneware, and marbled agate-ware with the appearance of tortoiseshell. His teapots appeared in the shapes of elephants, squirrels and camels in imitation of the Chinese habit of mythologising animals; and when he discovered a fine green glaze they were metamorphosed into cauliflowers and cabbages. His invention of creamware, an extra-fine smooth earthenware renamed Queensware when Queen Charlotte bought a set, appeared twice daily on thousands of English tea tables throughout the eighteenth century, for it was much cheaper than porcelain. Later he produced black Basalt, a fine-grained black earthenware, commenting on its dramatic effect at the tea table, 'I hope white hands will continue in fashion and then we may continue to make the Black teapot.' To the late eighteenth-century craze for everything classical, Wedgwood contributed his famous Jasperware, moulded white classical figures superimposed on to unglazed earthenware pots and cups the colour of sugared almonds (including the renowned light Wedgwood blue).

Victorian Worthies

After more than a century of drinking tea from China, the British instigated and won the disgraceful Opium Wars against the Chinese. The causes of these wars will not be explored any further here for fear of shocking the reader. Meanwhile tea had been found growing wild in India, and soon enormous quantities of the new black teas were pouring into Britain from various corners of her Empire. Eminent Victorians ensured the continuance of our national passion for tea. Lord Wellington was never without his silver teapot on campaigns. William Gladstone, four times Prime Minister under Queen Victoria, often boasted that he drank more tea between midnight and 4 a.m. than any other MP, and even claimed that his hot water bottle was filled with boiling Assam. Queen Victoria had a special Balmoral tea service made by Minton, with bright tartan borders. So popular was tea that the two-spouted teapot was invented (one spout poured from where the tea was infusing, and the other from another part of the pot for a weaker brew). Whiskery Victorians drank from Moustache Cups, which had a small ledge inside the brim upon which a moustache could rest without getting wet. Teapots appeared in all guises: as garish Majolica robins or monkeys; as miniature cathedrals during the neo-Gothic revival, complete with little knights and bishops in niches; and above all as vehicles for sentimental or commemorative messages like Forget Me Not and God Bless Our Queen.

Nor was there any longer a danger of ash leaves or sheep dung finding their way into the teapot. In 1826, honest Quaker John Horniman started to measure tea leaves into sealed paper packets with a guaranteed net weight before selling them, which was such a sensible idea that it became general practice. (Horniman was eventually bought out by two orphaned teenage brothers, the Tetleys, who had made some money peddling tea to inaccessible Yorkshire villages.) Tea was the star beverage at temper-

ance meetings of the 1830s, where, if at all possible, the tea-urn was manned by a reformed drunkard for maximum moral effect.

But tea had not become so safe and sober that it could no longer cut a dash. Speedy three-masted ships called clippers were built to bring cargoes of tea to Europe, and their races across the oceans of the world to be first up the Thames with the new season's tea inspired feverish bets and gambling on a national scale. The new steam ships combined with the time-saving Suez Canal to put a stop to the tea clippers in 1869.

The Invention of Afternoon Tea

Anna, 7th Duchess of Bedford, grew tired of the sinking feeling which afflicted her every afternoon round about 4 o'clock, in the long dull space of time between meals. In 1840 she plucked up courage and asked for a tray of tea, bread and butter, and cake to be brought to her room. Once she had formed the habit she found she could not break it, so spread it among her friends instead. As the century progressed, afternoon tea became increasingly elaborate. By the 1880s ladies were changing into long tea gowns for the occasion, appetites sharpened by the customary afternoon drive in a carriage. These tea gowns were soft, diaphanous, festooned with lace furbelows, and always suitably loose-waisted.

Tea services had also kept pace, with side plates, bread and butter plates, cake stands and every conceivable accompaniment advancing across the drawing room. There was a newly translucent delicacy about the tea china itself thanks to Josiah Spode, who had at the start of the century invented bone china, a beautiful and inexpensive form of porcelain which

ONE MAN, ONE TEAPOT

For once, the rich were not able to keep the best things to themselves. Tea jumped all barriers of class and income. Everybody in England was passionate for the beverage, to the point of depriving themselves of the necessaries of life in order to buy their twice-daily pots of tea.

* La Rochefoucauld wrote in 1784, 'Throughout the whole of England the drinking of tea is general. You have it twice a day and though the expense is considerable, the humblest peasant has his tea just like the rich man.'
* Erik Geijer, a young Swede visiting England in 1809, noted, 'Next to water tea is the Englishman's proper element. All classes consume it, and if one is out on the London streets early in the morning, one may see in many places small tables set up under the open sky, round which coal-carters and workmen empty their cups of the delicious beverage.'
* William Cobbett was infuriated by the fact that the average labourer spent something approaching a third of his earnings on tea, and denounced the beverage as a wicked waste of time and money. 'The tea drinking has done a great deal in bringing this nation into the state of misery in which it now is,' he fulminated in *Cottage Economy*, 1822. 'It must be evident to every one that the practice of tea drinking must render the frame feeble, and unfit to encounter hard labour or severe weather, while . . . it deducts from the means of replenishing the belly and covering the back. Hence succeeds a softness, an effeminacy, a seeking for the fire side, a lurking in the bed, and, in short, all the characteristics of idleness.'

kept tea hot even though it was so fine that you could see your fingers' shadows through it.

By Edwardian times, the smart hour for afternoon tea was five o'clock or later, and what had started as a little hiatus for refreshment had become a full-blown social occasion, with hot dishes, footmen handing round the teacups, and even professional musicians. Ornately encrusted silver teapots and huge silver tea urns on swivel stands lent weight to the event. Etiquette books full of anxious advice appeared, with warnings like 'those who take sugar in their tea are advised to propel the spoon with a minimum of effort and to remove it without fail before raising the cup'. Conversation was kept as sweet and lightweight as the teatime meringues. In Saki's short story *Tea*, the hero imagines his intended wife with something approaching horror: 'Joan would be seated at a low table, spread with an array of silver kettles and cream-jugs and delicate porcelain teacups, behind which her voice would tinkle pleasantly in a series of little friendly questions about weak or strong tea, how much, if any, sugar, milk, cream, and so forth. "Is it one lump? I forgot. You do take milk, don't you? Would you like some more hot water, if it's too strong?" '

Meanwhile the teashop flourished for lesser mortals. The Aerated Bread Company was the first, in 1864, to open shops where people could drink tea and eat cakes. The success of these ABC teashops was immediate and astounding. In their wake followed: teashops managed by the Express dairies; J. Lyons' red plush establishments with waitresses called

'nippies'; teashops within department stores (most notably Whiteley's, where a ladies' orchestra accompanied the tea drinking); Gunters; the Kardomah tea shops; and Fullers, with their legendary frosted walnut cakes. For a more elaborate and graceful tea, of course, you could always visit the Ritz.

Afternoon Tea Now

Afternoon tea has suffered something of a decline since the Second World War. This century's mania for thinness has done it a disservice by branding sandwiches and cakes Luciferan. Also, life has speeded up so that it is no longer easy to pause at four for tea. But tea has still not lost its symbolic or emotional status in England. Whenever anything momentous occurs, whether matter for celebration or tragedy, a pot of tea is produced. When friends meet unexpectedly, they exchange news over tea. There is a calming element of ceremonial about the whole affair which is too valuable to lose. Afternoon tea is still a graceful event, and brings people together for a brief hour's pleasure and refreshment.

Sandwiches and Savoury Dishes

fternoon tea must always start with sandwiches. You are not allowed to move on to the cakes and muffins until you have blunted the teeth of your appetite with a sandwich.

The obligatory sandwich, so ingenious and practical, was the brainchild and namesake of the fourth Earl of Sandwich. The daredevil Earl lived life, appropriately enough, on a knife edge, hurling his fortunes around at the gaming tables. His gambling sessions often lasted twenty-four hours or more, and one night in 1762, the rumbling from his stomach was so violent that his attention strayed dangerously from combinations of clubs and diamonds to chimeras of bread and meat. He had a good hand and could

not bear to rise for a meal. 'Stap me vitals,' he groaned. What could he do? This cruel dilemma produced an inspired solution. He whispered to his manservant, who returned, minutes later, with a hunk of beef between two slices of bread. The gamblers gasped at such brilliance. The Earl wolfed down the world's first sandwich, and that night won ten thousand pounds. Of all the constituents of afternoon tea, the sandwich has dated the least. This chapter describes several different teas tailor-made to individual requirements. Only bear in mind that the practical and nutritious sandwich is of paramount importance when afternoon tea becomes the last meal of the day.

The Archetypal Afternoon Tea

This reached its zenith on golden Edwardian afternoons, when tea appeared in a silver pot and the cucumber sandwich scaled the heights of immortality. It is now a graceful anachronism, although it might still be revived at weekends and on holidays. Mrs Humphrey gives a menu for just such a full-blown drawing-room tea in *Etiquette for Every Day* (1902), itemising tea, coffee, bread and butter, five kinds of sandwich, oyster *vol au vents*, chicken cutlets, two creams, four jellies, an ice, soft drinks and a claret cup. None but a purist would reproduce this menu now, though the spirit of the occasion can be captured with the help of a sense of theatre. Set the scene, arrange the props, and invite your wittiest, chattiest acquaintances. Bear in the tea things on a tray covered with a snowy cut-work cloth. Offer both Indian and China tea, and several plates of slim crustless sandwiches.

CUCUMBER SANDWICHES

Peel a cucumber and slice it into transparencies on the slicing side of a grater, or by adroit use of a potato peeler. Sprinkle these see-through discs with a little vinegar and salt. After half an hour, drain away the excess cucumber juice by shuffling the slices in a sieve. Cover a slice of lightly buttered paper-thin brown bread with two layers of cucumber, and top with another slice of bread. Apply firm but delicate pressure with the palm of the hand. Slice off the crusts, and cut into three rectangles. Pile these neatly on a porcelain serving plate, and cover with a lightly dampened cloth until tea is served.

THE CUCUMBER SANDWICH

The cucumber sandwich is the aristocrat of the teatable; cool, gracious and impeccable. Should you peel the cucumber or not? It depends on whether you like the thin green line (also upon whether or not you live in America, where cucumbers are waxed and therefore *must* be peeled). One thing is for certain—the bread must be as slim as a leaf. By virtue of its utter simplicity and symbolic status, the cucumber sandwich is also one of the few foods to rise from the merely culinary world to dizzy literary heights.

Algernon: *(picking up an empty plate in horror) Good heavens! Lane! Why are there no cucumber sandwiches? I ordered them specially.*

Lane: *(gravely) There were no cucumbers in the market this morning, sir. I went down twice.*

Algernon: *No cucumbers!*

Lane: *No, sir. Not even for ready money.*

Algernon: *That will do, Lane, thank you.*

From *The Importance of Being Earnest*,
Oscar Wilde

THE RITZ'S
SPECIAL EGG SANDWICHES

——METRIC/IMPERIAL—— •	——CUP MEASURES——
Mayonnaise	*Mayonnaise*
2 egg yolks (size 3)	2 medium egg yolks
10 ml/2 tsp English mustard powder	2 tsp dry English mustard
15 ml/1 tbsp Worcestershire sauce	1 tbsp Worcestershire sauce
2.5 ml/½ tsp salt	½ tsp salt
1.25 ml/¼ tsp white pepper	¼ tsp white pepper
200 ml/7 fl oz olive oil	scant cup olive oil
15 ml/1 tbsp lemon juice	1 tbsp lemon juice
Egg mixture	*Egg mixture*
5 eggs (size 3), hard-boiled and shelled	5 medium eggs, hard-boiled and shelled
dash of Tabasco (optional)	dash of hot pepper sauce (optional)
mustard and cress	cress

To make the mayonnaise, stir all the ingredients on the list, *except* for the oil and lemon juice, in a mixing bowl until well blended. Now beat this vigorously with a whisk, adding a few drops of oil at a time. Slowly but surely your mayonnaise will thicken. Add a little lemon juice to adjust the consistency and sharpen the taste. Chop the hard-boiled eggs roughly. Stir into the mayonnaise. Taste, and season with Tabasco or hot pepper sauce if you like a stronger flavour. Spread onto thinly-sliced buttered white bread, and top with a springy green cress coverlet. Press slices of buttered white bread on top, remove the crusts, and slice.

The Club Man's Tea

This tea is hearty and bluff, extremely savoury and accompanied by pints of steaming Assam tea. It would go down well after a hard day in the City. Earl Sandwich would have approved.

The Club Man's sandwiches are made with brown bread, not too thinly sliced. As to fillings, there are two perennial favourites. Patum Peperium, or Gentleman's Relish, is a sharp dark paste of eye-watering strength, made from anchovies, butter, herbs and spices. Spread it thinly and top with mustard and cress. The other classic sandwich filling of this type is made with generous slices of good pink ham spread with a skimming of hot mustard.

The Club Man also munches through stacks of hot buttered toast, which he likes to spread with potted shrimps.

POTTED SHRIMPS

——METRIC/IMPERIAL—— •	——CUP MEASURES——
225 g/8 oz peeled shrimps (or prawns)	½ lb shelled cooked shrimp
2.5 ml/½ tsp mace	½ tsp grated mace or nutmeg
1.25 ml/¼ tsp ground ginger	¼ tsp ground ginger
175 g/6 oz butter, melted	12 tbsp (1½ sticks) butter, melted
salt, black pepper and cayenne	salt, black pepper and cayenne

Chop half the shellfish finely. Mix the chopped and whole shellfish in a bowl with the mace, ginger and 100 g (4 oz) or 1 stick (8 tbsp) of the melted butter. Stir all this in a pan over a low heat and sprinkle with salt and pepper. Stir occasionally until the butter has been absorbed into the mixture. Pack it down well into little jars and pots. Clarify the rest of the butter by bringing to the boil and straining it through a piece of muslin or cheesecloth. Pour the hot butter over the potted shrimps and leave to cool. Add a smattering of cayenne pepper and chill in the refrigerator (where the mixture will keep for a month under its veil of clarified butter).

Since it so rarely appears at dinner any more, that most English of dishes, the savoury, may be added to the Club Man's tea. A savoury is very small, very hot and strongly flavoured. Considered suitable only for the male palate, this smidgeon of machismo was designed to precede the port at the end of a long dinner.

SCOTCH WOODCOCK

METRIC/IMPERIAL	CUP MEASURES
6 anchovy fillets	6 anchovy fillets
1.25 ml/¼ tsp black pepper	¼ tsp black pepper
2 slices of crustless, buttered toast, trimmed to 7.5 cm (3-inch) squares	2 slices of crustless, buttered toast trimmed to 3-inch squares
2 egg yolks (size 3)	2 medium egg yolks
20 ml/4 tsp double cream	4 tsp heavy cream
15 g/½ oz butter, melted	1 tbsp butter, melted

Pound the anchovy fillets with the black pepper and spread on the toast. Beat the egg yolks with the cream, and season well. Stir the butter into the creamy egg mixture until it begins to thicken. Pour over the toast and serve hot.

ENGLISH RABBIT

METRIC/IMPERIAL	CUP MEASURES
2 slices of white bread	2 slices of white bread
175 ml/6 fl oz claret	¾ cup red wine
25 g/1 oz butter	2 tbsp (¼ stick) butter
125 g/4 oz grated Cheddar cheese	1 cup grated Cheddar cheese
10 ml/2 tsp hot mustard	2 tsp spicy mustard

Place the slices of bread side by side in a dish and pour the wine over them. Allow it to soak in for a few minutes. Dot the wine-dark bread with half the butter and toast it fast on both sides. Melt the rest of the butter, cheese, mustard and any wine left over in the dish gently together; then, like greased lightning, spread this mixture over the toast and make it bubble under the grill or broiler.

DEVILLED HAM TOASTS

METRIC/IMPERIAL	•	CUP MEASURES
50 g/2 oz lean ham, finely chopped		$\frac{1}{3}$ cup finely chopped lean ham
10 ml/2 tsp Worcestershire sauce		2 tsp Worcestershire sauce
cayenne pepper		cayenne pepper
10 ml/2 tsp French mustard		2 tsp French mustard
15 g/$\frac{1}{2}$ oz butter		1 tbsp butter
4 slices of toast		4 slices of toast
15 ml/1 tbsp chopped fresh parsley		1 tbsp chopped fresh parsley

Cut a circle from each slice of toast with a sharp knife, using a tea cup as the template. Amalgamate the ham, Worcestershire sauce, cayenne and French mustard. Melt the butter in a small pan and stir in the mixture. Heat it until it starts to sizzle, then pile it onto the toast circles, crown with parsley, and serve immediately.

The Nursery Tea

It was once an iron rule that children must eat bread-and-butter and sandwiches before cake; and that they should not have more than two slices of cake, generally only one, and then only two or three times a week. Tea can be made into a treat for children by cutting sandwiches into little squares and triangles and including

Winter Teas

The English, and particularly English find it comforting to draw the curtain on a n afternoon sky, turning with relief to an fire in front of which they toast and butter little delicacy for themselves. This action omething positive-spirited and rotective about it, they n obscurely, like hares growing cker coat or ormouse ng up for nation. ens' cters, so of- nd them- s making provision st winter, are ys making and devouring pets. Every care- ictorian furnished his son with a brass toasting fork and a silver muffin dish for afternoons in college rooms and later at the Club. 'Don't worry, my boy,' the good father would advise, 'The noble art of toasting is easy, not nearly as bad as learning how to boil an egg.' Thomas de Quincy set the scene perfectly: 'Surely every one is aware of the divine pleasures which attend a wintry fireside: candles at four o'clock, warm hearthrugs, tea, a fair tea-maker, shutters closed, curtains flowing in ample draperies to the floor, whilst the wind and rain are raging audibly without.'

the occasional sweet sandwich filling.

Sardine sandwiches have been a favourite for generations. Mash some drained tinned sardines with a fork. Add a couple of squeezes of lemon juice. Butter thinly-sliced brown bread, spread with the sharply-flavoured sardine paste and cover with the second buttered slice. Cut the crusts off. Forget that nonsense about crusts making your hair curl; today's child is not so easily taken in.

Banana sandwiches are sweet and satisfying. Peel and mash a banana with a couple of table-spoons of cream and two teaspoons of soft brown sugar. Spread this on crustless white bread.

The classic sandwich of American childhood is the 'peanut-butter-and-jelly'. This savoury-sweet hybrid is made by spreading one slice of bread with peanut butter and slapping it against another slice spread with strawberry jam. If your tastebuds are British and you cannot bring yourself to do this, try substituting redcurrant jelly for the jam. Once introduced to this, certain children will eat nothing else.

TOMATO SANDWICHES

Skin some hard young tomatoes by steeping them in boiling water for a minute, draining them, and then sliding them out of their jackets. Slice them thinly with a knife so sharp that it does not drag any seeds from the inside tracery. Arrange the slices on thin lightly-buttered bread (brown, because it looks so fine beside the rosy tomatoes). Grind a few flakes of black pepper over this before topping with another slice.

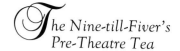

The Nine-till-Fiver's Pre-Theatre Tea

If you work during the day and flit around for pleasure in the evening, there will come a low point in your energy. This is usually at about 6.30 p.m., when it is tempting to swallow a gin-and-tonic or a bar of chocolate as there is no time to cook a proper meal. This is exactly where a light swiftly-prepared tea is ideal. Also, drinking tea itself will revive and enliven, and the effect of the caffeine will have worn off by the time you are ready for sleep. The best pre-theatre tea recipes involve sustaining ingredients like cheese, eggs, or smoked salmon.

WELSH RAREBIT

This is also known as Welsh Rabbit (probably the correct form, as old French recipe books name the recipe *Lapin Gallois*), though all but pedants prefer to say 'rarebit' these days.

METRIC/IMPERIAL	CUP MEASURES
125 g/4 oz grated cheese, Lancashire for preference	1 cup grated sharp Cheddar cheese
45 ml/3 tbsp ale	3 tbsp dark ale
25 g/1 oz butter	2 tbsp ($\frac{1}{4}$ stick) butter
5 ml/1 tsp hot mustard	1 tsp spicy mustard
salt and black pepper	salt and black pepper
2 slices of toast	2 slices of toast

Melt the cheese and ale in a small pan over a low heat. Add the butter and mustard. Sprinkle in salt and black pepper. Pour the cheese onto the toast and grill or broil until the cheese bubbles and almost starts to scorch in patches.

SCRAMBLED EGGS WITH SMOKED SALMON

METRIC/IMPERIAL	CUP MEASURES
15 g/½ oz butter	1 tbsp butter
2 eggs (size 3), lightly beaten	2 medium eggs, lightly beaten
15 ml/1 tbsp milk	1 tbsp milk
black pepper	black pepper
25 g/1 oz smoked salmon offcuts, finely snipped	2 tbsp finely chopped smoked salmon trimmings
1 slice brown toast	1 slice brown toast

Melt the butter to foaming point and pour in the lightly-beaten eggs and milk seasoned with black pepper. Nudge the curds around gently over a low heat with a wooden spoon. Throw in the scraps of salmon when you turn the heat off, so that they join the eggs during those few mysterious seconds when the cooking process appears to continue on its own and the eggs become more set than liquid. Spoon onto the toast in a generous mound, and serve.

Sandwiches should be surprising and delicious, to put you in the right state of mind for an evening's enjoyment.

WATERCRESS SANDWICH

These are bright, peppery, crisp and full of iron. Butter rough rye bread with salty butter and pile a slice high with fresh watercress. Press another slice on top until the contents creak. Cut the sandwich in half but not quarters... the dark green leaves burst out at the seams.

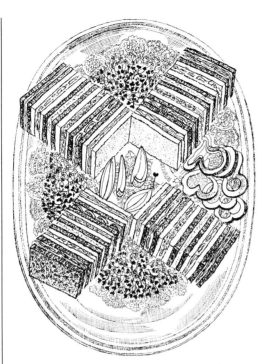

THE ALICE B. TOKLAS SANDWICH

Poach two or three large chopped mushrooms in butter with a little lemon juice for about eight minutes. Remove from the heat and mash, then beat to a paste. Add salt, pepper, a few grains of cayenne, and a roughly equal volume of softened butter. For variety, Miss Toklas would beat in a scrambled egg and grated Parmesan cheese too; she believed that these additions made the sandwich filling even more delicious, so that it tasted almost like chicken.

THE RITZ'S SPECIAL SMOKED SALMON SANDWICHES

METRIC/IMPERIAL	CUP MEASURES
100 g/4 oz smoked salmon offcuts	¼ lb smoked salmon trimmings
150 ml/¼ pint single cream	1⅓ cups heavy cream
25 ml/1 fl oz whisky	2 tbsp whisky
2.5 ml/½ tsp white pepper, plus extra	½ tsp white pepper, plus extra
1.25 ml/¼ tsp grated nutmeg	¼ tsp grated nutmeg
150 ml/¼ pint double cream	brown bread-and-butter
brown bread-and-butter	2 oz slice smoked salmon, cut wafer thin
50 g/2 oz slice smoked salmon, cut wafer thin	lemon wedge, to serve
lemon wedge, to serve	

Mince or chop the smoked sa[...]
Stir in the single or ⅔ cup of [...]
coax the mixture through a [...]
using the back of a wooden sp[...]
whisky, pepper and nutmeg. C[...]

Whip the double or remain[...] until stiff, and fold into the cl[...] little at a time. Spread slice[...] bread-and-butter with the mi[...] fully arrange wafers of smoke[...] this. Season with a little fresh[...] pepper. Press slices of buttered[...] top and remove the crusts. C[...] wiches with a clean cloth which[...] out in cold water until you ar[...] them. Serve with a wedge of le[...]

This makes an exceptionally [...] sandwich.

THE MAD HATTER'S TEA PARTY

'Have some wine', the March Hare said in an encouraging tone. Alice looked all round the table, but there was nothing on it but tea.
'I don't see any wine', she remarked.
'There isn't any', said the March Hare.
   Lewis Carroll, *Alice in Wonderland*

STRIPED SANDWICHES

Take one white loaf and one brown loaf. Cut each loaf into long horizontal slices.

Butter each slice on one side [...] with a thin layer of cream chees[...] their crusts with a bread knife. [...] striped loaf by pressing the cr[...] and brown slices together in alte[...] Press the slices together firmly[...] chill. To serve, cut the bread i[...] inch) wide striped fingers.

PITTA POCKETS ZAZ[...]

Slice pitta breads across the wa[...] in an oven until they open easil[...] crumbled stilton, broken walnu[...] slices of a ripe Comice pear.

TOAST IN DICKENS

'The fire was blazing brightly under the influence of the bellows, and the kettle was singing gaily under the influence of both. A small tray of tea-things was arranged on the table, a plate of hot buttered toast was gently simmering before the fire, and the red-nosed man himself was busily engaged in converting a large slice of bread into the same agreeable edible, through the instrumentality of a long brass toasting-fork.'

Charles Dickens, *Pickwick Papers*

Toast

Impale your 5 mm (¼ inch) slice of white bread on a brass toasting fork and hold its face near the flames of a good coal or log fire. When the required shade of gold (turning almost to brown) has been reached, toast the other side. Butter generously and immediately, so that the butter melts and sinks in; cut in half and pile toast on a plate which you keep warm by the fireside. Cover it with an earthenware bowl if you have one. If you do not have an open fire, use your oven grill or broiler to make toast. The electric toaster destroys the lyricism of this occasion, combining with bread to form a bland marriage of convenience, and producing toast of a sameness and uniformity which kills appetite.

CINNAMON TOAST

METRIC/IMPERIAL	CUP MEASURES
15 ml/1 tbsp ground cinnamon	1 tbsp ground cinnamon
30 ml/2 tbsp caster sugar	2 tbsp superfine sugar
several rounds hot buttered toast	several slices hot buttered toast

Mix the spice and sugar, and sprinkle on to the toast.

CRUMPETS

Crumpets are straight-sided, pale, round and hot, honeycombed with holes, ideal for absorbing butter. They are made from a thin batter poured into rings on a hot griddle. (Pikelets, which come from Derbyshire and Yorkshire, are very like crumpets but they are flatter, cooked without rings, and do not have such good holes.)

METRIC/IMPERIAL	CUP MEASURES
225 g/8 oz plain flour	3 cups unbleached flour
10 ml/2 tsp salt	2 tsp salt
225 g/8 oz strong plain flour	1¼ cups milk mixed with 1¼ cups water
300 ml/½ pint milk mixed with 300 ml/½ pint water	2 tbsp vegetable oil
30 ml/2 tbsp oil	1 tsp sugar
5 ml/1 tsp sugar	2 tsp active dry yeast
15 g/½ oz fresh or 2 tsp dried yeast	½ tsp baking soda
2.5 ml/½ tsp bicarbonate of soda	7 tbsp warm water
100 ml/4 fl oz warm water	

Crumpet rings 7.5–10 cm (3–4 inches) wide × 2.5 cm (1 inch) deep, greased
Makes 8–10 crumpets

Sift the flour and salt into a warm bowl, cover, and place in a very low oven for ten minutes. Warm the milk, water, oil and sugar, then add 60 ml/4 tbsp/¼ cup of this to the yeast, which should soon froth and go creamy. If using dried yeast, stir the yeast into all the liquid and leave in a warm place until frothy. Make a well in the centre of the warmed flour, and pour in the yeast mixture, then the rest of the liquid, if any. Stir and beat the batter energetically for a good five minutes, incorporating as much air as possible. Cover the bowl and leave it for two hours at warm room temperature, until the surface is covered with bubbles. Dissolve the bicarbonate of soda or baking soda in 2–3 tbsp warm water and stir it into the batter, beating for another couple of minutes. Cover the bowl again and leave it for another hour.

Lightly grease a griddle, large heavy frying pan or skillet with lard or shortening. Place the crumpet rings on the griddle, some three or four at a time, filling each ring almost to the top with the mixture, and heat gently for eight to ten minutes until the surface becomes pitted with holes. Slip the rings off and turn the crumpets over to cook for another four minutes. You can either butter them immediately and eat them while hot, or save them to toast on both sides a little later. N.B. If holes do not appear in your first batch as markedly as you would wish, add a little warm water to the rest of the batter and your remaining crumpets will be properly labyrinthine.

THE ART OF BUTTERING CRUMPETS

'All crumpets should be toasted on both sides, the smooth side first, the holey side last, as this produces a suitable concavity for the butter. . . . Never cut a muffin, snip round the curved side and pull top and bottom apart and insert the butter in thin slices, do not attempt to spread it.'
Dorothy Hartley, *Food in England*

AND MUFFINS

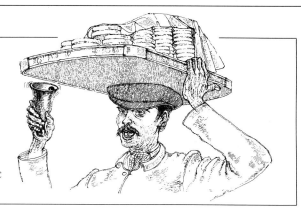

'Muffins should not be split and toasted. The correct way to serve them is, to open them slightly at their joint all the way round, toast them back and front, tear them open and butter the insides liberally. Serve hot.'

Marian McNeill, *The Book of Breakfast*

ENGLISH MUFFINS

These are made with a stiffer batter than crumpets, and are baked without rings. They do not have holes. Grown men become extremely emotional about them, especially over the matter of how they should be buttered.

——METRIC/IMPERIAL—— • ——CUP MEASURES——	
450 g/1 lb strong plain flour	3 cups unbleached flour
10 ml/2 tsp salt	2 tsp salt
175 ml/6 fl oz water mixed with 175 ml/ 6 fl oz milk	$\frac{3}{4}$ cup water mixed with $\frac{3}{4}$ cup milk
30 ml/2 tbsp olive oil	2 tbsp olive oil
15 g/$\frac{1}{2}$ oz fresh or 2 tsp dried yeast	2 tsp active dry yeast
5 ml/1 tsp sugar	1 tsp sugar
rice flour for dusting	rice flour for dusting

Makes 8 muffins

Sift the flour and salt into a bowl, then cover and place in a very low oven. Gently warm the water and milk and olive oil (until tepid). Cream the yeast and sugar with a few spoonfuls of this liquid. If using dried yeast, stir the yeast into all the liquid and leave in a warm place until frothy. Make a well in the middle of the warmed flour and pour in the yeast followed by the rest of the liquid, if any. Stir, then knead. The dough should be very slack and soft, but not sticky. Cover the bowl with a damp cloth and leave it in a warm room for about an hour, until the dough has grown to twice its size. Divide it in half, then into quarters, and finally into eight pieces. Mould each piece into a globe, and flatten slightly with the heel of your palm. Dust all over with rice flour. Put them on a well-floured board and cover with a cloth for forty minutes so that they swell again. Heat a lightly greased griddle or skillet and transfer the muffins as carefully as if they were rare birds' eggs, using a fish slice or pancake turner. Cook them gently for eight minutes on each side. They will look floury, pale gold-brown, white-waisted, and should be anything up to 5 cm (2 inches) thick. Toast them, butter them, and take them to the table hot, if possible in an old-fashioned covered muffin-dish with hot-water compartment.

TEA CAKES

METRIC/IMPERIAL	CUP MEASURES
25 g/1 oz butter	2 tbsp (¼ stick) butter
450 g/1 lb plain flour	3 cups unbleached flour
5 ml/1 tsp salt	1 tsp salt
15 g/½ oz fresh or 2 tsp dried yeast	2 tsp active dry yeast
5 ml/1 tsp caster sugar	1 tsp superfine sugar
300 ml/½ pint milk at blood heat	1¼ cups warm milk
75 g/3 oz sultanas and currants, mixed	½ cup golden raisins and currants, mixed
5 ml/1 tsp sugar dissolved in 30 ml/ 2 tbsp milk for glaze	1 tsp sugar dissolved in 2 tbsp milk for glaze

Oven: 400°F/200°C/Mark 6
Makes 6 tea cakes

Butter two baking sheets. In a large mixing bowl rub or cut the butter into the sifted flour and salt. Stand the covered bowl in a warm place. Cream the yeast with the sugar and a little of the warmed milk, and leave it to froth for twenty minutes. If using dried yeast, stir the yeast into all the warmed milk and leave in a warm place until frothy. Uncover the bowl and make a well in the flour, then pour in the yeast and enough of the warm milk to make a soft elastic dough. If using dried yeast, pour in all the liquid. Stir the flour in from the sides and knead well for 10 minutes. Mix in the fruit. Cover, and leave to prove in a warm place for an hour or so until twice the size. Pull the dough into six pieces, and shape and knead each piece into a round, slightly flattened cake about 10 cm (4 inches) in diameter. Arrange on the baking sheets. Prick with a fork, cover with a cloth, and leave to rise for 15 minutes. Bake for 20 minutes. When the tea cakes emerge from the oven, give them a shine by brushing very lightly with the glaze. Serve hot, split in two and buttered; or, toasted top and bottom, split, then toasted inside, buttered, sandwiched together again and sliced into quarters.

THE MAGIC INGREDIENT: YEAST

'The bowl was put on the hearth, covered with a white cloth and left to rise. It took about an hour or a little longer and everyone had a peep under the cloth to see how it was getting on. A child would poke a finger in it and be reprimanded. Dough was exciting, a lively white cushion, growing bigger and bigger.'

Alison Uttley,
Recipes from an Old Farmhouse

the occasional sweet sandwich filling.

Sardine sandwiches have been a favourite for generations. Mash some drained tinned sardines with a fork. Add a couple of squeezes of lemon juice. Butter thinly-sliced brown bread, spread with the sharply-flavoured sardine paste and cover with the second buttered slice. Cut the crusts off. Forget that nonsense about crusts making your hair curl; today's child is not so easily taken in.

Banana sandwiches are sweet and satisfying. Peel and mash a banana with a couple of tablespoons of cream and two teaspoons of soft brown sugar. Spread this on crustless white bread.

The classic sandwich of American childhood is the 'peanut-butter-and-jelly'. This savoury-sweet hybrid is made by spreading one slice of bread with peanut butter and slapping it against another slice spread with strawberry jam. If your tastebuds are British and you cannot bring yourself to do this, try substituting redcurrant jelly for the jam. Once introduced to this, certain children will eat nothing else.

TOMATO SANDWICHES

Skin some hard young tomatoes by steeping them in boiling water for a minute, draining them, and then sliding them out of their jackets. Slice them thinly with a knife so sharp that it does not drag any seeds from the inside tracery. Arrange the slices on thin lightly-buttered bread (brown, because it looks so fine beside the rosy tomatoes). Grind a few flakes of black pepper over this before topping with another slice.

The Nine-till-Fiver's Pre-Theatre Tea

If you work during the day and flit around for pleasure in the evening, there will come a low point in your energy. This is usually at about 6.30 p.m., when it is tempting to swallow a gin-and-tonic or a bar of chocolate as there is no time to cook a proper meal. This is exactly where a light swiftly-prepared tea is ideal. Also, drinking tea itself will revive and enliven, and the effect of the caffeine will have worn off by the time you are ready for sleep. The best pre-theatre tea recipes involve sustaining ingredients like cheese, eggs, or smoked salmon.

WELSH RAREBIT

This is also known as Welsh Rabbit (probably the correct form, as old French recipe books name the recipe *Lapin Gallois*), though all but pedants prefer to say 'rarebit' these days.

METRIC/IMPERIAL	CUP MEASURES
125 g/4 oz grated cheese, Lancashire for preference	1 cup grated sharp Cheddar cheese
45 ml/3 tbsp ale	3 tbsp dark ale
25 g/1 oz butter	2 tbsp (¼ stick) butter
5 ml/1 tsp hot mustard	1 tsp spicy mustard
salt and black pepper	salt and black pepper
2 slices of toast	2 slices of toast

Melt the cheese and ale in a small pan over a low heat. Add the butter and mustard. Sprinkle in salt and black pepper. Pour the cheese onto the toast and grill or broil until the cheese bubbles and almost starts to scorch in patches.

SCRAMBLED EGGS WITH SMOKED SALMON

METRIC/IMPERIAL	CUP MEASURES
15 g/½ oz butter	1 tbsp butter
2 eggs (size 3), lightly beaten	2 medium eggs, lightly beaten
15 ml/1 tbsp milk	1 tbsp milk
black pepper	black pepper
25 g/1 oz smoked salmon offcuts, finely snipped	2 tbsp finely chopped smoked salmon trimmings
1 slice brown toast	1 slice brown toast

Melt the butter to foaming point and pour in the lightly-beaten eggs and milk seasoned with black pepper. Nudge the curds around gently over a low heat with a wooden spoon. Throw in the scraps of salmon when you turn the heat off, so that they join the eggs during those few mysterious seconds when the cooking process appears to continue on its own and the eggs become more set than liquid. Spoon onto the toast in a generous mound, and serve.

Sandwiches should be surprising and delicious, to put you in the right state of mind for an evening's enjoyment.

WATERCRESS SANDWICH

These are bright, peppery, crisp and full of iron. Butter rough rye bread with salty butter and pile a slice high with fresh watercress. Press another slice on top until the contents creak. Cut the sandwich in half but not quarters...the dark green leaves burst out at the seams.

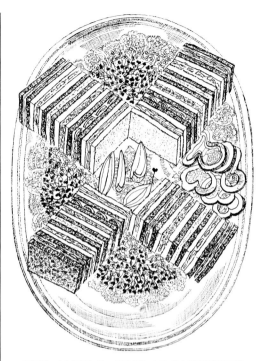

THE ALICE B. TOKLAS SANDWICH

Poach two or three large chopped mushrooms in butter with a little lemon juice for about eight minutes. Remove from the heat and mash, then beat to a paste. Add salt, pepper, a few grains of cayenne, and a roughly equal volume of softened butter. For variety, Miss Toklas would beat in a scrambled egg and grated Parmesan cheese too; she believed that these additions made the sandwich filling even more delicious, so that it tasted almost like chicken.

THE RITZ'S SPECIAL
SMOKED SALMON SANDWICHES

——METRIC/IMPERIAL—— •	——CUP MEASURES——
100 g/4 oz smoked salmon offcuts	¼ lb smoked salmon trimmings
150 ml/¼ pint single cream	1⅓ cups heavy cream
25 ml/1 fl oz whisky	2 tbsp whisky
2.5 ml/½ tsp white pepper, plus extra	½ tsp white pepper, plus extra
1.25 ml/¼ tsp grated nutmeg	¼ tsp grated nutmeg
150 ml/¼ pint double cream	brown bread-and-butter
brown bread-and-butter	2 oz slice smoked salmon, cut wafer thin
50 g/2 oz slice smoked salmon, cut wafer thin	lemon wedge, to serve
lemon wedge, to serve	

Mince or chop the smoked salmon very finely. Stir in the single or ⅔ cup of heavy cream, and coax the mixture through a sieve or strainer using the back of a wooden spoon. Beat in the whisky, pepper and nutmeg. Chill.

Whip the double or remaining heavy cream until stiff, and fold into the chilled mixture, a little at a time. Spread slices of the brown bread-and-butter with the mixture, then carefully arrange wafers of smoked salmon across this. Season with a little freshly-ground white pepper. Press slices of buttered brown bread on top and remove the crusts. Cover the sandwiches with a clean cloth which has been wrung out in cold water until you are ready to serve them. Serve with a wedge of lemon.

This makes an exceptionally moist delicious sandwich.

THE MAD HATTER'S
TEA PARTY

'Have some wine', the March Hare said in an encouraging tone. Alice looked all round the table, but there was nothing on it but tea.
'I don't see any wine', she remarked.
'There isn't any', said the March Hare.
     Lewis Carroll, *Alice in Wonderland*

STRIPED SANDWICHES

Take one white loaf and one brown loaf. Cut each loaf into long horizontal slices. Butter each slice on one side and spread with a thin layer of cream cheese. Saw off all their crusts with a bread knife. Build a new striped loaf by pressing the crustless white and brown slices together in alternate layers. Press the slices together firmly, wrap and chill. To serve, cut the bread into 7.5 cm (3 inch) wide striped fingers.

PITTA POCKETS ZAZOU

Slice pitta breads across the waist and heat in an oven until they open easily. Stuff with crumbled stilton, broken walnuts and thin slices of a ripe Comice pear.

Winter Teas

The English, and particularly English men, find it comforting to draw the curtain on a leaden afternoon sky, turning with relief to an open fire in front of which they toast and butter some little delicacy for themselves. This action has something positive-spirited and self-protective about it, they reason obscurely, like arctic hares growing a thicker coat or the dormouse curling up for hibernation. Dickens' characters, who so often find themselves making cosy provision against winter, are always making toast and devouring crumpets. Every careful Victorian furnished his son with a brass toasting fork and a silver muffin dish for afternoons in college rooms and later at the Club. 'Don't worry, my boy,' the good father would advise, 'The noble art of toasting is easy, not nearly as bad as learning how to boil an egg.' Thomas de Quincy set the scene perfectly: 'Surely every one is aware of the divine pleasures which attend a wintry fireside: candles at four o'clock, warm hearthrugs, tea, a fair tea-maker, shutters closed, curtains flowing in ample draperies to the floor, whilst the wind and rain are raging audibly without.'

DROP SCONES OR SCOTCH PANCAKES

These are the simplest and quickest of all hot little cakes. They are made without yeast, but are still very light.

——METRIC/IMPERIAL——	——CUP MEASURES——
225 g/8 oz plain flour	1½ cups unbleached flour
2.5 g/½ tsp bicarbonate of soda	½ tsp baking soda
5 ml/1 tsp cream of tartar	1 tsp cream of tartar
2.5 ml/½ tsp salt	½ tsp salt
1 egg, (size 3), beaten	1 medium egg, beaten
300 ml/½ pint milk	1¼ cups milk
15 ml/1 tbsp caster sugar	1 tbsp sugar

Makes 30 drop scones

Sift the flour, bicarbonate of soda or baking soda, cream of tartar and salt all together. Beat together the egg, milk and sugar. Stir this into the flour a little at a time until you have a thick batter. Drop dessertspoonfuls of the batter onto a hot lightly-greased griddle, heavy frying pan or skillet, holding the point of the spoon downwards. Cook until bubbles show on top. Flip the flat cakes over and cook for the same amount of time on the other side. They will only need two or three minutes cooking on each side. As you finish each batch, slide them off the griddle with a palette knife or spatula onto a hot plate covered with a cloth napkin, and keep them covered. Serve them well-buttered and as soon as possible.

A waiting audience is best.

English Cakes

In England it is possible to have your cake and eat it without being in turn consumed by guilt. This is because English cakes are plain, elegant and wholesome. They may be eaten not only at the tea table but also as part of lunch or at the end of dinner. Continental and American cakes are made to look positively wicked by comparison. English cakes are respectable.

Before you bake any cake, however modest, there are certain things to bear in mind. First and most important, cakes are highly responsive to the mood of their makers. If you are in a hurry or a fluster, if you do not really want to be making a cake, the cake will know it and behave accordingly. It will toughen and grow heavy-hearted and its fruit will drop within it. Never ever open the oven door before the appointed time as the cake, discouraged by the cold air of the outside world, will sink in the middle. Cakes are so sensitive that they lapse immediately into sadness if lack of confidence in their progress is shown. They must be allowed to cook as slowly as they like, and prefer the middle shelf of the oven. Every cake should be a planned cake, which means that you will have thought to remove any necessary ingredients from the refrigerator well in advance; this way, all will be at room temperature when you approach the mixing bowl.

At the dawn of the admirably reasonable eighteenth century, English cooks discovered how to make plain light cakes. They found that by adding eggs to creamed butter and sugar they could create a mixture just strong enough to support a handful of ground almonds, a little desiccated or shredded coconut or a sprinkling of caraway seeds. (They had relied on yeast till this point, even using it in their great rich fruit cakes.) The result was a delicately-flavoured cake, easily digestible, a model of demure restraint, perfect with a glass of sherry or sweet wine. Afternoon tea had not been invented at this stage, but, when it was, these ubiquitous cakes persisted. They have remained firm English favourites to this day.

MADEIRA CAKE

Modest and moist-textured, this cake earned its name because it was served mid-morning with a glass of the sweet malmsey wine from Madeira. It is a teetotaler itself, entirely safe for children and temperance workers, as its ingredients will show. Its sole vanity is the traditional crowning ornament of citron peel, translucent and jade-coloured.

METRIC/IMPERIAL •	CUP MEASURES
175 g/6 oz butter	12 tbsp (1½ sticks) butter
175 g/6 oz caster sugar	¾ cup sugar
15 g/½ oz ground almonds	1 tbsp ground almonds
3 eggs (size 3), beaten	3 medium eggs, beaten
175 g/6 oz self raising flour	1½ cups self-rising flour
grated rind of 1½ lemons	grated peel of 1½ lemons
2 large slices citron peel	2 large slices citron peel

Oven: 325°F/170°C/Mark 3
18 cm (7 inch) round cake tin, 8.5 cm (3½ inches) deep
Makes one cake

Grease and line the tin. Cream the butter and sugar together until light and fluffy. Sprinkle in the almonds and stir. Add the eggs a little at a time, beating well all the time. Fold in the flour; stir and scatter the lemon rind or peel in too.

Transfer the mixture to the tin and bake for an hour. Taking care that there will be no sudden draughts, slide out the oven shelf and position the two strips of citron peel on the dome of the cake. Bake for another half hour. Allow the cake to cool in its tin for several minutes before carefully turning it out onto a wire rack.

COCONUT CAKE

METRIC/IMPERIAL •	CUP MEASURES
125 g/4 oz butter	8 tbsp (1 stick) butter
125 g/4 oz caster sugar	½ cup sugar
3 eggs (size 3), beaten	3 medium eggs, beaten
200 g/7 oz self raising flour	1¼ cups self-rising flour
50 g/2 oz desiccated coconut	⅔ cup shredded coconut
finely grated rind and juice of ½ lemon	finely grated rind and juice of ½ lemon

Oven: 350°F/180°C/Mark 4
18 cm (7 inch) round cake tin, 8.5 cm (3½ inches) deep
Makes one cake

Grease and line the cake tin. Cream the butter and sugar until fluffy. Beat in the eggs gradually and rhythmically. Fold in the flour, sifting from on high, then stir in the coconut, lemon rind and juice. Scoop this batter into the cake tin. Bake for 1¼ hours. Cool the cake in its tin for a few minutes, then transfer to a wire rack to cool completely.

If you like, before sliding it into the oven, you may scatter across the top of the cake a mixture of a tablespoon of desiccated or shredded coconut with 15 ml/½ tbsp of caster or superfine sugar. During baking this will form a slight sweet crust.

SEED CAKE

This has existed in various forms since the Middle Ages, and was one of England's most popular cakes until Edwardian times, when, unaccountably, it fell from favour. Modern cake-eaters may not be accustomed to the austere flavour and hardness of the seeds against the edge of their teeth, but it is time this surprising, refreshing and foolproof cake regained its popularity.

METRIC/IMPERIAL	CUP MEASURES
125 g/4 oz butter	8 tbsp (1 stick) butter
150 g/5 oz caster sugar	$\frac{2}{3}$ cup sugar
2 eggs (size 2), beaten	2 large eggs, beaten
10 ml/2 tsp caraway seeds	2 tsp caraway seeds
150 g/5 oz plain flour	$1\frac{1}{4}$ cups unbleached flour
25 g/1 oz cornflour	3 tbsp cornstarch
2.5 ml/$\frac{1}{2}$ tsp baking powder	$\frac{1}{4}$ tsp baking powder
5 ml/1 tsp ground cinnamon	1 tsp ground cinnamon
1.25 ml/$\frac{1}{4}$ tsp ground cloves	$\frac{1}{4}$ tsp ground cloves

Oven: 350°F/180°C/Mark 4
15 cm (6 inch) round cake tin, 7.5 cm (3 inches) deep
Makes one cake

Grease and line the tin. Cream the butter and sugar until there is no grittiness. Work in the caraway seeds. Beat in the eggs a little at a time. Stir together the remaining ingredients, then fold them in too, with a metal spoon. Turn this mixture carefully into the tin. Bake for $1\frac{1}{4}$ hours. Leave to cool for a few minutes in the tin, then carefully turn out onto a wire rack.

THE LITERARY SEED CAKE

'Miss Lavinia and Miss Clarissa partook, in their way, of my joy. It was the pleasantest tea-table in the world. Miss Clarissa presided. I cut and handed the sweet seed-cake—the little sisters had a bird-like fondness for picking up seeds and pecking at sugar; Miss Lavinia looked on with benignant patronage, as if our happy love were all her work; and we were perfectly contented with ourselves and one another.'

Charles Dickens, *David Copperfield*

MARBLE CAKE

This was a great favourite with the Victorians. It is named not for its weight—it is an airy cake—but for its appearance. When cut, each slice shows the feathered swirling of Italian Carrara marble or marbled endpapers.

——METRIC/IMPERIAL—— •	——CUP MEASURES——
175 g/6 oz butter	12 tbsp (1½ sticks) butter
175 g/6 oz caster sugar	¾ cup sugar
3 eggs (size 3), beaten	3 medium eggs, beaten
175 g/6 oz self raising flour	1¼ cups self-rising flour
50 g/2 oz plain chocolate, melted and kept warm	2 squares semi-sweet chocolate, melted and kept warm

Oven: 350°F/180°C/Mark 4
18 cm (7 inch) round cake tin, 8.5 cm (3½ inches) deep
Makes one cake

Grease and line the cake tin with greaseproof or wax paper.

Cream together the butter and sugar until pale and thick, then gradually beat in the eggs, beating well after each addition. Sift the flour over the surface and gently fold in.

At this point, it is necessary to make a choice. If you are a safe cook, divide the batter between two bowls and add the melted chocolate to one of these, beating well. Drop spoonfuls of the batters into the tin, alternating the plain with the chocolate. Use the handle of a wooden spoon to give one quick swirl, then bake for 1¼ hours.

Alternatively, if you are brave and generally behave with *élan*, leave the batter in one bowl.

Trickle the melted chocolate in three lines over the surface, then wave a knife blade back and forth through these lines. Take great care that the pale batter is streaked but not so thoroughly mixed as to look muddy with chocolate. You will have to trust your eye and sleight of hand. Bake for 1¼ hours.

Cool the cake in its tin for a few minutes then transfer to a wire rack to cool completely.
NOTE: The tame cook's cake will look cloudy and its marbled markings will be pale and more solid. The daring cook's cake will be cream-coloured and feathered with chocolate streaks, like the marbled endpapers of an old book. Whichever you choose, both cakes taste delicious.

Use only the best quality of chocolate as this makes a great difference to the flavour of the cake.

Sponge Cakes

These are perhaps the most temperamental and sensitive of all cakes. They were not seen in English kitchens until the end of the eighteenth century, when it became possible to maintain the constant oven temperature so essential to their success. Even so, in the days when eggs were beaten with a fork or a bunch of birch twigs, you did not lightly undertake to bake a sponge cake. Recipes would carry the instruction, 'beat eggs for three hours.' Metal balloon whisks made things easier for Mrs Beeton and her generation. In 1932, patriotic tradition-loving cookery writer Florence White wrote a passage in praise of the new electric egg-whisk: 'So the past and the present have clasped hands and never the twain shall part; and arm-aching produced by whisking eggs, whipping cream, or making sillabubs is known no more. But the invention is American. Those cousins of ours are so clever.' (*Good Things in England*)

CLASSIC FATLESS SPONGE

This puffs up like a golden cloud, but must be eaten within a couple of hours of emerging from the oven. It grows sad after that, and is good for nothing but to sop up juices in a trifle.

METRIC/IMPERIAL	CUP MEASURES
3 eggs (size 3)	3 medium eggs
75 g/3 oz caster sugar	6 tbsp sugar
75 g/3 oz plain flour, sifted with a pinch of salt three times	$\frac{1}{2}$ cup cake flour, sifted with a pinch of salt three times
icing sugar for dusting	confectioners' sugar for dusting

Oven: 350°F/180°C/Mark 4
18 cm (7 inch) round cake tin, 7.5 cm (3 inches) deep.
Makes one cake

Lightly butter the cake tin. Sprinkle it inside with a spoonful of sugar sifted with a spoonful of flour; tap sharply upside down. If beating the eggs by hand, take a warmed mixing bowl and set it over a pan of hot (but not boiling) water. Whisk the eggs and sugar together in this until creamy and voluminous, then remove from heat and beat for a few more minutes until even bulkier. (If using an electric mixer, whisk for 2 minutes at the highest speed.) With a metal spoon, fold in the flour and salt as delicately as possible. Swiftly pour the mixture into the cake tin. Bake for 45 minutes. Remove from the tin and place on a wire rack to cool.

Do not meddle with it beyond lightly dusting the surface with icing or confectioners' sugar. Use restraint, serve immediately, and the natural delicacy and aristocratic taste of this cake will appear.

VICTORIA SANDWICH

This was named in honour of Queen Victoria, who relished the new craze for tea-parties. The invention of baking powder in 1855 meant that there was no longer need for lengthy egg beating, and baking cakes became a much easier business altogether as a result. Here, butter is added to the classic sponge mixture, resulting in a more substantial cake which keeps for a day or two. Simple to make, it should be every child's first recipe.

METRIC/IMPERIAL •	CUP MEASURES
100 g/4 oz butter	8 tbsp (1 stick) butter
100 g/4 oz caster sugar	$\frac{1}{2}$ cup sugar
2 eggs (size 3), beaten	2 medium eggs, beaten
100 g/4 oz self raising flour	1 cup self-rising flour
Filling	*Filling*
60 ml/4 tbsp strawberry jam	4 tbsp strawberry jam
150 ml/¼ pint whipped cream (optional)	⅔ cup heavy cream (optional)

Oven: 375°F/190°C/Mark 5
Two 18 cm (7 inch) sandwich or layer cake tins
Makes one cake

Lightly butter the cake tins and line with grease-proof or wax paper. Cream the butter and sugar until light and fluffy. Add the eggs gradually, beating well. Sift the flour and fold it in with a large metal spoon. Stir lightly but thoroughly. Turn the mixture into the tins and smooth the tops with a palette knife or spatula for evenness. Bake for 20 minutes. When cool, sandwich together with strawberry jam and maybe whipped cream as well.

Delicious Heirlooms
BRANDY SNAPS

These were sold at medieval fairs, when they were known as gauffres or wafers. They are crisp curls of toffee-coloured laciness, slightly hot-flavoured from the smidgeon of ginger.

METRIC/IMPERIAL •	CUP MEASURES
50 g/2 oz butter	4 tbsp (½ stick) butter
50 g/2 oz demerara sugar	¼ cup soft light brown sugar
50 g/2 oz golden syrup	4 tbsp corn syrup
2.5 ml/½ tsp ground ginger	½ tsp ground ginger
50 g/2 oz plain flour, sifted	½ cup unbleached flour, sifted
2.5 ml/½ tsp lemon juice	½ tsp lemon juice

Oven: 425°F/220°C/Mark 7
Makes 10 brandy snaps

Line two baking sheets with non-stick or parchment paper. Gently warm the butter, sugar, syrup and ginger in a thick-based saucepan until the butter has melted and you have a syrupy liquid. Add the sifted flour and lemon juice. Take generous teaspoonfuls of the mixture and tap them out, five round dollops to each baking sheet, spaced well apart. Bake for 15 minutes; they will spread into malleable lacy discs. Before they cool to hardness, lift each in turn with a palette knife or spatula and roll it cleverly around the handle of a greased wooden spoon. These curls cool fast on a wire rack. They are lovely on their own, or meltingly delicious if filled at each end with whipped cream containing tiny fragments of preserved ginger and a spoonful of the ginger syrup.

FRUIT CAKE

Fruit cake, the richest of English cakes, was called plum cake for centuries although nobody can fathom why as it never contained plums, nor even prunes. These plum cakes held pounds and pounds of cut peel and dried fruit...raisins, sultanas or golden raisins and particularly currants (for which this island has shown a violent fondness since Roman times)...all supported in a yeast dough and baked in freehand shapes or metal hoops in the old bread-ovens.

This modern version is infallible and densely-fruited. You may prefer to substitute for the mixed peel and some of the fruit, equal weights of chopped prunes, chopped dried apricots, chopped dried apples, and some chopped preserved ginger.

METRIC/IMPERIAL •	CUP MEASURES
225 g/8 oz sultanas	1⅓ cups seedless golden raisins
225 g/8 oz raisins	1⅓ cups raisins
225 g/8 oz currants	1⅓ cups currants
225 g/8 oz strong plain flour	1½ cups unbleached flour
5 g/1 tsp baking powder	½ tsp baking powder
225 g/8 oz butter, softened	½ lb (2 sticks) butter, softened
225 g/8 oz caster sugar	1 cup sugar
4 eggs (size 3), beaten	4 medium eggs, beaten
50 g/2 oz mixed candied peel	⅓ cup mixed candied peel
grated rind of 1 lemon	grated rind of 1 lemon

Oven: 325°F/170°C/Mark 3
18 cm (7 inch) round cake tin, 8.5 cm (3½ inches) deep
Makes one cake

The lion and the unicorn
Were fighting for the crown;
The lion beat the unicorn
All round the town.
Some gave them white bread,
And some gave them brown;
And some gave them plum cake,
And sent them out of town.

(Old Nursery Rhyme)

The dried fruit should all have been soaked in cold water for an hour to plump it; drained well in a sieve and dried by spreading on a baking sheet covered with foil and placed in a warm oven for 5 minutes; then coated in a mixture of a few tablespoons of flour from the main quantity with the baking powder added.

Butter and line the tin with greaseproof or wax paper. Cream the butter and sugar together by hand until you can feel the sugar has lost its grittiness. Beat in the eggs, a little at a time, with a wooden spoon. Be thorough here. Fold in half the flour with a metal spoon, a little at a time. Add the evenly-mixed dried fruit, mixed peel and lemon rind, then the rest of the flour. Stir. Scoop the mixture into the tin. Level the top, and make a slight depression in the middle with the back of a spoon.

Bake for four hours. Test the cake after this time by pressing it in the middle with your fingertips. It should feel firm and slightly springy to the touch. Or plunge a bright, *hot*, shiny skewer into its heart; if this emerges still shining, not sticky, the cake is cooked. One last test is to lift it from the oven and listen to it, placing your ear to its side. If you can hear it singing away to itself inside, it is not cooked. And if in doubt, it is better slightly to overcook than to undercook a fruit cake. Remove from the oven and allow to cool for half an hour or longer in its tin, leaving it to settle itself somewhat. Turn onto a wire rack and cool further. When quite cold, store in an airtight tin where it will last for a long time. Even impatient people should not cut the first slice till six weeks have passed.

Foreign Cakes and Wicked Cakes

All the cakes in this chapter are culinary *emigrés* which have succeeded in winning over plain English cooks to their delectable foreign ways. Rich tea-table morsels began to creep across from the Continent during Victoria's reign, while the triple-decker fudge-iced extravaganzas of America arrived a little later. Such cakes hold a frisson of wickedness for the English cook, as they glory in quantities of cream and chocolate and tooth-deep frosting. Sweet sirens of the cake world, they are smooth and rich as film stars.

To begin with, though, there are two famous *friandises* which manage to combine delicious-ness with an unusually virtuous simplicity.

MADELEINES

These are little French sponge cakes which look, as Proust described them, as though they had been moulded in the fluted valve of a scallop shell. Each cake, he maintained, was richly sensual under its severe religious folds. Traditional madeleine tins have long shell-shaped indentations; you can use shallow jam tart tins or muffin tins instead, but these lack poetry.

The faint lemon flavour of madeleines is intensified when they are eaten with lime blossom (*tilleul*) tea.

THE MADELEINE AS AIDE-MEMOIRE

Marcel Proust tastes a madeleine dipped in tea in that most famous moment of all in *Remembrance of Things Past*.

'And as in the game wherein the Japanese amuse themselves by filling a porcelain bowl with water and steeping in it little pieces of paper which until then are without character or form, but, the moment they become wet, stretch and twist and take on colour and distinctive shape, become flowers or houses or people, solid and recognisable, so in that moment all the flowers in our garden and in M. Swann's park, and the water-lilies on the Vivonne and the good folk of the village and their little dwellings and the parish church and the whole of Combray and its surroundings, taking shape and solidity, sprang into being, town and gardens alike, from my cup of tea.'

——METRIC/IMPERIAL—— •	——CUP MEASURES——
2 eggs (size 3), separated	2 medium eggs, separated
100 g/4 oz caster sugar	$\frac{1}{2}$ cup sugar
100 g/4 oz unsalted butter, melted	8 tbsp (1 stick) unsalted butter, melted
finely grated rind and juice of $\frac{1}{2}$ lemon	finely grated rind and juice of $\frac{1}{2}$ lemon
100 g/4 oz self raising flour	$\frac{1}{2}$ cup self-rising flour

Oven: 375°F/190°C/Mark 5
Two trays of madeleine, jam tart or muffin tins
Makes about 24 madeleines

Lightly butter the madeleine tins.

Beat the egg yolks and sugar until they are thoroughly mixed but still bright yellow. Beat in the melted butter, lemon rind and juice, then sift the flour over the surface and fold in. Stir the egg whites with a fork; then beat them well into the mixture.

Spoon a small amount of the mixture into each mould and bake in the centre of the oven for 20 minutes. Cool slightly in the moulds before gently easing out onto wire racks to cool completely. These are best eaten very fresh.

MACAROONS

These flat round almond biscuits were first made in Greece, then became a Neapolitan delicacy in the tenth century, reaching England some seven hundred years later. Long-enduring favourites, they are still popular.

They are best stored in an airtight tin between layers of greaseproof or wax paper.

——METRIC/IMPERIAL—— •	——CUP MEASURES——
225 g/8 oz caster sugar	1 cup sugar
100 g/4 oz ground almonds	1 cup ground almonds
10 ml/2 tsp ground rice	2 tsp corn starch
2–3 drops natural almond essence	2–3 drops natural almond extract
5 ml/1 tsp orange flower water	1 tsp orange flower water
2 egg whites (size 3)	2 medium egg whites
10 almonds, blanched and split	10 almonds, blanched and split
edible rice paper	edible rice paper

Oven: 350°F/180°C/Mark 4
Makes 20 macaroons

Line two baking sheets with edible rice paper. Mix together the sugar, ground almonds and ground rice or corn starch, and sprinkle in the natural almond essence or extract and orange flower water. Stir the egg whites with a fork, then add them to the mixture a little at a time, mixing to a fairly stiff paste. Beat well. Pinch off small pieces of paste, roll into little spheres, and arrange these on the rice paper, allowing space for spreading between each. Flatten each sphere slightly with the heel of your hand. Lightly brush their crowns with water to give a glaze. Press a split almond on top of each macaroon. Bake for 20–25 minutes until pale gold-brown. Cool on a wire rack, then tear the rice paper from around the border of each macaroon. They will be crisp outside, with a crackled surface and a slightly chewy heart.

MERINGUES

Meringues are frivolous little French cakes, fragile and as light as feathers. It is a relief to learn they escape the censure dealt to the cake family by nineteenth-century cookery writer Eliza Acton, who wrote, 'more illness is caused by habitual indulgence in the richer and heavier kinds of cake than could easily be credited by persons who have given no attention to the subject.' Meringues, however, she exonerated, as, 'being extremely light and delicate, and made of white of egg and sugar only, (they) are really not unwholesome.' They are so light that they sound hollow when tapped.

The meringues served for tea at the Ritz are frail pink and white shells joined with whipped cream and crowned with slices of fruit.

——METRIC/IMPERIAL——	——CUP MEASURES——
4 egg whites (size 3)	4 medium egg whites
225 g/8 oz caster sugar	1 cup sugar
2–3 drops cochineal	2–3 drops red food colouring
300 ml/½ pint double cream, whipped	1¼ cups heavy cream, whipped
flour for dusting	flour for dusting
fresh fruit in season for decoration	fresh fruit in season for decoration

Oven: 200°F/100°C/Mark ¼
Makes 16 half cases

Grease two baking sheets and dust them with flour. Whisk the egg whites until they are at the cumulus cloud stage, standing in stiff snowy peaks. Sift 75 g/3 oz/6 tbsp of the sugar over their surface and whisk again until the mixture grows glossy and like satin. Add the remaining sugar, folding in a little at a time with a metal spoon. Transfer half the mixture to another bowl, and stir in two or three drops of the red food colouring to this until it blushes pale pink. Now, using a large star nozzle and piping or pastry bag, pipe the meringue mixture in lengths of about 10 cm (4 inches), with a spiralling movement of the wrist. Pipe the white mixture onto one baking sheet and the pink onto the other. Bake for four hours.

When they are completely cold, sandwich them flat sides together, a pink shell to every white one, with whipped cream. Arrange on a plate so that they rest along one creamy seam. Along the top line of cream which now presents itself to your eye, arrange three pieces of fruit. A slice of kiwi fruit and a sliver of pineapple look good with a black cherry still on its stalk, but choose from whatever is in season.

FLORENTINES

METRIC/IMPERIAL	CUP MEASURES
90 g/3½ oz butter	7 tbsp butter
100 g/4 oz caster sugar	½ cup sugar
100 g/4 oz flaked almonds, chopped	⅔ cup chopped slivered almonds
50 g/2 oz sultanas	⅓ cup golden raisins
6 glacé cherries, chopped	6 candied cherries, chopped
25 g/1 oz cut mixed peel	2 tbsp chopped candied mixed peel
15 ml/1 tbsp single cream	1 tbsp heavy cream
175 g/6 oz plain chocolate	6 squares semi-sweet chocolate

Oven: 350°F/180°C/Mark 4
Makes about 12 Florentines

Line three baking sheets with non-stick or parchment paper. In a large pan melt the butter, stir in the sugar, and boil them together for one minute. Remove the pan from the heat. Stir in the rest of the ingredients, except for the chocolate, until all of them are coated in hot syrupy stickiness. Drop small rounded heaps of the mixture onto the baking sheets. Keep them well apart, one to each corner of every baking sheet, to allow room for spreading. Bake for ten minutes until toast-coloured.

Nudge the edges of each Florentine into a roughly circular shape with the blade of a palette knife or spatula. Leave on the baking sheets for five minutes until they start to harden. Transfer them to a wire rack; take care here, as this is the most difficult step of the procedure. Leave to cool. Meanwhile, melt the chocolate in a heatproof bowl over a saucepan of boiling water. Give the flat side of each Florentine a generous brown coat of melted chocolate. Make even wavy patterns in the chocolate with the prongs of a fork. Leave to set hard.

BROWNIES

These rich fudgy chocolate squares have been firm favourites with generations of American children.

——METRIC/IMPERIAL—— •	——CUP MEASURES——
125 g/4 oz plain chocolate	4 squares semi-sweet chocolate
50 g/2 oz butter	4 tbsp ($\frac{1}{2}$ stick) butter
2 eggs (size 3)	2 medium eggs
175 g/6 oz caster sugar	$\frac{3}{4}$ cup sugar
5 ml/1 tsp natural vanilla essence	1 tsp vanilla extract
75 g/3 oz self raising flour	$\frac{1}{2}$ cup self-rising flour
50 g/2 oz walnuts, roughly chopped	$\frac{1}{3}$ cup roughly chopped walnuts

Oven: 350°F/180°C/Mark 4
20.5 cm (8 inch) square cake tin
Makes 9 big squares or 16 smaller ones

Butter and line the tin with non-stick or parchment paper. Melt the chocolate in a heatproof bowl over boiling water. Slice the butter roughly into the warm chocolate and stir until this melts too. Remove from the heat and allow to cool.

Beat the eggs, sugar and vanilla essence together, stir them into the chocolate mixture, and beat again. Fold in the flour with a large metal spoon. Stir in the walnuts. Spoon or pour the mixture into the tin and bake for 25–40 minutes (depending on how fudgey and gooey you like them). Cool for 10 minutes, then cut into squares. Turn out onto a wire rack. A pale flakey autumn-leaf surface will form on top.

PANFORTE

This is a delectable Italian cake studded with nuts and citrus rinds, flat, hard and fragrant with honey. It takes a determined glutton to consume more than one wedge of its dense richness at one sitting.

——METRIC/IMPERIAL—— •	——CUP MEASURES——
50 g/2 oz almonds	$\frac{1}{3}$ cup almonds
50 g/2 oz hazelnuts	$\frac{1}{3}$ cup hazelnuts
50 g/2 oz candied orange peel, chopped	$\frac{1}{3}$ cup chopped candied orange peel
50 g/2 oz candied lemon peel, chopped	$\frac{1}{3}$ cup chopped candied lemon peel
10 ml/2 tsp ground cinnamon	2 tsp ground cinnamon
50 g/2 oz plain flour	$\frac{1}{2}$ cup unbleached flour
65 g/$2\frac{1}{2}$ oz honey	5 tbsp honey
65 g/$2\frac{1}{2}$ oz soft brown sugar	5 tbsp soft light brown sugar
icing sugar	confectioners' sugar
rice paper	rice paper

Oven: 300°F/150°C/Mark 2
18 cm (7 inch) sandwich or layer cake tin with removable base
Makes one cake

Line the base and edges of the tin with rice paper. Blanch the almonds in boiling water, then slip them out of their coats. Toast the almonds and hazelnuts on a baking tray in a low oven for several minutes, the hazelnuts still in their brown skins. Remove from the oven. Blow and pinch the hazelnut skins away. Chop the nuts together quite finely. Mix together with the citrus rinds, cinnamon and flour until evenly mingled. Heat the honey and sugar until they start to boil, then trickle them into the main nutty fruity mixture, stirring all the while. Using a wooden spoon, press this fragrant mass into the prepared tin. Bake for 30 minutes. Cool in tin, then remove and sprinkle the surface with icing or confectioners' sugar. This keeps well when wrapped in foil.

DEVIL'S FOOD CAKE

This American chocolate cake has no rival for sybaritic exuberance. An essential element is its thick sandwiching of chocolate fudge frosting.

METRIC/IMPERIAL	CUP MEASURES
75 g/3 oz plain chocolate	3 squares semi-sweet chocolate
350 g/12 oz soft brown sugar	1½ cups soft light brown sugar
45 ml/3 tbsp dark rum	3 tbsp dark rum
125 g/4 oz butter	8 tbsp (1 stick) butter
2 eggs (size 3), beaten	2 medium eggs, beaten
225 g/8 oz self raising flour	2 cups self-rising flour
60 ml/4 tbsp milk	¼ cup milk
Frosting	*Frosting*
50 g/2 oz plain chocolate	2 squares semi-sweet chocolate
50 g/2 oz butter	4 tbsp (½ stick) butter
350 g/12 oz icing sugar	3 cups confectioners' sugar
30 ml/2 tbsp strong coffee	2 tbsp strong coffee
30 ml/2 tbsp single cream	2 tbsp light cream

Oven: 350°F/180°C/Mark 4
Three 20.5 cm (8 inch) sandwich or layer cake tins
Makes one cake

Grease the tins and line with greaseproof or wax paper. Heat together over the lowest possible heat in a thick-based saucepan the chocolate, half the sugar, and the rum, stirring until smooth. Put aside to cool. Cream the butter with the rest of the sugar and gradually beat in the eggs. Add the chocolate mixture and beat again. Stir in the flour and milk, a little at a time. Divide this mixture between the three sandwich tins. Bake for 30–35 minutes. Allow the cakes to cool in their tins for five minutes, then turn them out onto a wire rack.

Melt the chocolate and butter together carefully, without letting them become too hot. Remove from the heat, then gradually stir in half the icing or confectioners' sugar, and the coffee, and beat until smooth. Add the rest of the sugar and the cream gradually, stirring then beating again.

Sandwich the cakes together with two layers of the chocolate fudge frosting. If you are very sweet-toothed, make double the quantity of frosting and cover the sides and top of the cake with it as well.

High Tea

Unlike afternoon tea, high tea is not a dainty affair. It usefully divides day from night, being held at six o'clock, rather than at the more idle and elegant afternoon-tea hour of four to five. It is hearty enough to make dinner unnecessary.

High tea still reigns in the north of England and Scotland, particularly in country regions. With any luck, it is a cheerful noisy gathering of family, friends and children after the day's work. Farmhouse high teas are the best, where the table bears a cornucopia of everything simple and fresh, and appetites are sharp set from working out in the air all day.

What You Will Find At High Tea: a large table spread with a white cloth; a heavy brown Firestone teapot pouring tea strong enough, as they say, to trot a mouse on; a side of smoked ham, perhaps, or an egg-and-bacon pie; a generous wedge of cheese; a dish of tomatoes and a bunch of watercress; some savoury dish like potted shrimps or even jugged kippers; scrambled eggs; bread-and-butter with pots of jam and honey; a plate of sandwiches; hot toasted tea cakes; and appetite-cutting cakes, often baked from recipes unique to the region, full of dried fruit and oatmeal and ginger.

What You Will NOT Find At High

Tea: delicate pretty cakes like mille feuilles or meringues; frosted confections; creamy gâteaux; little fingers crooked over teacups; silver teapots and fine porcelain; social chit-chat.

ROCK CAKES

These little cakes have a rough and craggy appearance, but are short and sweet to taste.

METRIC/IMPERIAL	CUP MEASURES
50 g/2 oz butter	4 tbsp (½ stick) butter
50 g/2 oz lard	¼ cup shortening
225 g/8 oz self raising flour	1½ cups self-rising flour
pinch of salt	pinch of salt
100 g/4 oz caster sugar	½ cup sugar
100 g/4 oz currants	⅔ cup currants
1 egg (size 3)	1 medium egg
about 15 ml/1 tbsp milk	1 tbsp milk

Oven: 400°F/200°C/Mark 6
Makes 12 rock cakes

Grease two baking sheets.

Rub or cut the butter and lard or shortening into the flour mixed with the salt, until you have a crumb-like texture. Stir in the sugar and currants with a knife until you have a well-mixed speckled mixture.

Beat the egg with a tablespoon or so of milk and add it, mixing with a fork until the mixture is rather stiff. Drop dessertspoonfuls of this onto the baking sheets. Bake for 15–20 minutes until lightly browned. Transfer to a wire tray to cool.

These are hardy delicious cakes, ideal for packing into a picnic basket.

FLAPJACKS

METRIC/IMPERIAL	CUP MEASURES
175 g/6 oz butter	12 tbsp (1½ sticks) butter
175 g/6 oz demerara sugar	¾ cup packed soft light brown sugar
45 ml/3 tbsp golden syrup	3 tbsp light corn syrup
225 g/8 oz rolled oats	2¼ cups oatmeal
pinch of salt	pinch of salt

Oven: 400°F/200°C/Mark 6
Shallow tin 20.5 × 30.5 cm (8 × 12 inches)—a Swiss roll or jelly roll tin does very well here
Makes 10–12 flapjacks

Lightly butter the tin or jelly roll pan. Melt the butter, sugar and syrup together over a gentle heat in a heavy saucepan. Mix the oats and salt, and trickle the melted ingredients over them, stirring all together. Turn this mixture into the tin and press it down evenly with the back of a wooden spoon. Bake for 20–25 minutes. Allow to cool for five minutes, then mark out squares with a sharp knife and leave in the tin until quite cold.

ECCLES CAKES

Eccles is a Lancashire town, and originally its name meant 'church'. These little currant-filled pastry cakes were made in Eccles on religious feast days. The Puritans decided they were too rich and delicious and probably secretly pagan into the bargain; they passed a law in 1650 which meant that you could be sent to prison for eating an Eccles cake. Now, fortunately, Eccles cakes are quite legal and just as delicious as before, particularly when served hot.

METRIC/IMPERIAL	CUP MEASURES
175 g/6 oz currants	1 cup currants
200 g/7 oz puff pastry (½ quantity) (page 9)	½ quantity (1 sheet frozen) puff pastry (page 9)
125 g/4 oz caster sugar	½ cup sugar
a little milk and caster sugar for glazing	a little milk and sugar for glazing

Oven: 425°F/220°C/Mark 7
Makes 9–10 Eccles cakes

Grease a baking sheet. Pour boiling water over the currants, enough to cover them; this will plump them up. Leave them to steep. Meanwhile, roll out the pastry quite thinly until it is about 30.5 cm (12 inches) square. This will be made easier if you roll the pastry between large sheets of greaseproof or wax paper. Stamp out 10 cm (4 inch) rounds with a cutter (or large cup or dish of that diameter). Strain the water from the currants; stir the sugar in with them. Place a little spoonful of this mixture in the middle of each pastry circle. Damp the circle's edges with water, and draw them together, pinching and nipping them closed, so that the pastry circle has become a pouchy little bag of currants. Turn the bag over and with a rolling pin gently press the cake so that its diameter grows to 7.5–10 cm (3–4 inches) again. You will see the shadow of the currants through their pastry veil. Brush over one side, the better-looking smoother side, with a little milk, then press it onto a board thinly sprinkled with sugar. On this glazed sugared surface make three parallel slits with the tip of a sharp knife (these are said to have represented the Holy Trinity) and the currants will peep through them. Bake for 15–20 minutes, until golden.

SHORTBREAD

Every Scots cook has his or her own recipe for this buttery crumbling Scottish biscuit-cake, disagreeing over the proportion of butter to flour, some forming it into solid fingers and others into thin triangles. A few like to add flavour; Mrs Beeton, for example, added caraway seeds and almonds to her shortbread mixture.

But most prefer their shortbread plain and honest.

METRIC/IMPERIAL	CUP MEASURES
50 g/2 oz caster sugar	¼ cup sugar
125 g/4 oz butter	4 tbsp (½ stick) butter
25 g/1 oz rice flour, sifted	2 tbsp rice flour, sifted
200 g/7 oz plain flour, sifted	1½ cups unbleached flour, sifted (add 2 more tbsp if rice flour unavailable)

Oven: 375°F/190°C/Mark 5
Rectangular tin 18–20.5 cm (7–8 inches) × 30.5 cm (12 inches)
Makes 24 shortbread fingers

Butter the tin. Cream the sugar and butter together with more than usual thoroughness. Combine the rice flour and the plain flour by sieving them together twice. Stir in the flours with more than usual lightness, until the mixture looks like fine breadcrumbs. Knead well until smooth. Pack and press it into the tin. Prick it all over with a fork. Bake for 45 minutes until very pale gold in colour. While still warm, dust with fine caster or superfine sugar and mark into oblong fingers.

Shortbread keeps for several weeks in an airtight tin.

DUNDEE CAKE

Dundee became famous for its marmalade in the eighteenth century. Even the dark light-textured fruitcake named after the city used to contain marmalade, and now candied orange peel and other citrus rinds are included as a reminder of this. The faces of Dundee cakes are paved concentrically with blanched almonds.

METRIC/IMPERIAL	CUP MEASURES
225 g/8 oz butter	½ lb (2 sticks) butter
225 g/8 oz soft brown sugar	1 cup soft light brown sugar
5 eggs (size 3), beaten	5 medium eggs, beaten
275 g/10 oz plain flour, sifted	2½ cups unbleached flour, sifted
225 g/8 oz currants	1⅓ cups currants
225 g/8 oz sultanas	1⅓ cups golden raisins
50 g/2 oz glacé cherries, cut in half	⅓ cup halved candied cherries
50 g/2 oz flaked almonds	⅓ cup slivered almonds
50 g/2 oz candied orange peel	⅓ cup candied orange peel
50 g/2 oz ground almonds	½ cup ground almonds
grated rind of 1½ oranges and ½ lemon	grated rind of 1½ oranges and ½ lemon
pinch of salt	pinch of salt
1.25 ml/¼ tsp bicarbonate of soda dissolved in 5 ml/1 tsp milk	¼ tsp baking soda dissolved in 1 tsp milk
50 g/2 oz blanched almonds, split lengthwise in halves	⅓ cup blanched almonds, split lengthwise in halves

Oven: 300°F/150°C/Mark 2
20.5 cm (8 inch) round cake tin, 7.5 cm (3 inches) deep
Makes one cake

Butter and line the tin with greaseproof or wax paper. Cream the butter and sugar in a large mixing bowl. Beat in a quarter of the eggs to the creamed mixture, then a quarter of the flour, repeating in turn like this until you have added all, making sure that the mixture is smooth and growing thicker after each addition. Stir in the fruit, flaked or slivered almonds, candied peel, ground almonds, grated rind and salt. Now add the soda dissolved in the milk, and stir it in well. Turn this bulky mixture into the tin. Stud the top of the cake with split almonds, split side down, starting at the middle and making rings outwards. Bake for 3½ hours. Leave to settle itself for half an hour, then turn out onto a wire rack to cool.

Gingerbreads

Gingerbread is one of the world's oldest cakes, and has been popular in England ever since the early days when it was made with honey and flavoured with claret, liquorice and pepper. They used to gild gingerbread for religious feasts (you can still do this with edible gold leaf from artists' stores, using unbeaten eggwhite as glue); roll it out with patterned rolling pins; or cut it into the shapes of saints and princes. Now we have gingerbread husbands instead, with currant buttons and iced eyebrows.

GINGERBREAD HUSBANDS

METRIC/IMPERIAL	CUP MEASURES
225 g/8 oz brown sugar	1 cup dark brown sugar
100 g/4 oz honey	⅓ cup honey
grated rind of 1 lemon	grated rind of 1 lemon
75 g/3 oz butter, diced	¾ stick (6 tbsp) butter, diced
225 g/8 oz plain flour	2 cups unbleached flour
5 ml/1 tsp baking powder	½ tsp baking powder
10 ml/2 tsp ground ginger	2 tsp ground ginger
45 ml/3 tbsp icing sugar	3 tbsp confectioners' sugar
few drops lemon juice	few drops lemon juice
currants for decoration	currants for decoration

Oven: 300°F/150°C/Mark 2
Makes 15 gingerbread husbands

> Run, run as fast as you can!
> You can't catch me!
> I'm the gingerbread man!

Butter two baking sheets. Warm the sugar, honey and lemon rind slowly over a low heat until the sugar has dissolved. Simmer for five minutes more. Add the butter to the hot pan. Stir until it melts. Remove from the heat. Stir in the flour, baking powder and ginger. Mix to a fairly stiff dough, and roll this out thinly on a floured board. Use a man-shaped cutter to press out shapes, or cut your own free-form men. Do not try to give them hands or feet! Press in currant eyes and a row of currant buttons. Transfer them to the baking sheets with a palette knife or spatula. Bake for 20 minutes. Carefully transfer them to a wire rack to cool. When they are cold, make some icing by dissolving the icing or confectioners' sugar in a few drops of the lemon juice. Apply it with a wooden cocktail stick, giving each little man curved eyebrows, a smile, and maybe even checked trousers or a Norfolk jacket, depending on how ambitious you are.

HELEN'S RICH GINGERBREAD

METRIC/IMPERIAL	CUP MEASURES
225 g/8 oz butter	½ lb (2 sticks) butter
225 g/8 oz dark brown sugar	1 cup dark brown sugar
2 eggs (size 3), beaten	2 medium eggs, lightly beaten
125 g/4 oz golden syrup	⅓ cup light corn syrup
125 g/4 oz black treacle	⅓ cup molasses
350 g/12 oz strong plain flour	2½ cups unbleached flour
5 ml/1 tsp ground mixed spice	1 tsp mixed ground cinnamon and nutmeg
10 ml/2 tsp ground ginger	2 tsp ground ginger
10 ml/2 tsp ground coriander	2 tsp ground coriander seeds
2.5 ml/½ tsp ground cloves	½ tsp ground cloves
225 g/8 oz sultanas, soaked, drained, and dusted in flour and baking powder	1⅓ cups golden raisins, soaked, drained and dusted in flour and baking powder
50 g/2 oz chopped preserved ginger	⅓ cup chopped candied ginger
grated rinds of 1 lemon and 2 oranges	grated rinds of 1 lemon and 2 oranges
250 ml/scant ½ pint milk	scant 1¼ cups milk
10 ml/2 tsp bicarbonate of soda	2 tsp baking soda

Oven: 325°F/170°C/Mark 3
Rectangular tin 20.5 cm × 30.5 cm (8 × 12 inches) ×
5 cm (2 inches) deep
Makes one cake

Butter and line the cake tin. Cream the butter and sugar together. Mix in the eggs, syrup and treacle or molasses. Sift the flour and spices into this fragrant syrup, stirring all the while.

Stir in the sultanas or golden raisins, ginger and grated citrus rinds. The mixture will be fairly stiff. Gently warm the milk and dissolve the bicarbonate of soda or baking soda in it. Stir this well into the main dark mixture. Transfer the batter to the prepared tin and bake for 1½ hours. Allow it to cool for a short while in the tin before turning it out onto the rack.

GRANTHAM GINGERBREADS

These are pale, hollow Georgian biscuits from Lincolnshire, crisp enough to make noisy eating and light enough to tempt a jaded appetite.

METRIC/IMPERIAL	CUP MEASURES
100 g/4 oz butter	8 tbsp (1 stick) butter
100 g/4 oz caster sugar	½ cup sugar
1 egg (size 3)	1 medium egg
225 g/8 oz plain flour, sifted	1½ cups unbleached flour, sifted
pinch of salt	pinch of salt
25 ml/½ tsp bicarbonate of soda	½ tsp baking soda
5 ml/1 tsp ground ginger	1 tsp ground ginger

Oven: 325°F/170°C/Mark 3
Makes 24 biscuits

Butter three baking sheets. Cream together the butter and sugar, and beat in the egg. Work the sifted flour, salt, bicarbonate of soda or baking soda and ginger into the creamed mixture. Turn this doughy mass onto a floured board and knead lightly until it is smooth. Form into 24 little spheres, rolling them between the palms of your hands. Place them on the baking sheets, allowing room for them to spread. Bake for thirty minutes until pale gold. Transfer them to a wire rack and allow to cool.

Summer Teas

*G*olden summer afternoons in England are now scarce and fleeting, possessing the same umbra of mythicality as unicorns. It is rumoured that they disappeared with the long hot summer of 1914. Certainly since that date writers have treated the hot, still sun-filled afternoon with yearning nostalgia as some *rara avis* from a lost domain. This tendency began with Rupert Brooke's famously wistful words,

'Stands the church clock at ten to three? And is there honey still for tea?'

The fact of the matter is that summer teas crop up all over England, quietly and enjoyably, at the slightest gleam of sunshine, wherever there is a garden, or a cricket pavilion, or a Women's Institute (where there will be excellent jam as well as honey for tea). Summer teas flourish most vigorously in the West Country, which has the best of the English weather. You cannot visit Devon or Cornwall without sampling the famous Cream Tea, with scones, jam, and clotted cream the rich colour of yellow garden roses.

If unable to buy clotted cream, double or heavy, whipped to a slightly-grained bulk like raw silk is a fair substitute. Long live the strawberry season and the summer tea!

The unhurried prose of Henry James gives fitting expression to a leisurely summer tea.

'Under certain circumstances there are few hours in life more agreeable than the hour dedicated to the ceremony known as afternoon tea. There are circumstances in which, whether you partake of the tea or not—some people of course never do—the situation is in itself delightful. Those that I have in mind in beginning to unfold this simple history offered an admirable setting to an innocent pastime. The implements of the little feast had been disposed upon the lawn of an old English country house in what I should call the perfect middle of a splendid summer afternoon. Part of the afternoon had waned, but much of it was left, and what was left was of the finest and rarest quality. Real dusk would not arrive for many hours; but the flood of summer light had begun to ebb, the air had grown mellow, the shadows were long upon the smooth, dense turf. They lengthened slowly, however, and the scene expressed that sense of leisure still to come which is perhaps the chief source of one's enjoyment of such a scene at such an hour. From five o'clock to eight is on certain occasions a little eternity; but on such an occasion as this the interval could be only an eternity of pleasure.'
Opening words of *The Portrait of a Lady* by Henry James

The Novice's Guide to Making Jam

Preserve summer in glass jars. Make jam. Home-made jam is entirely different from its commercial counterpart, and is the first pre-requisite of a summer tea. It is a pleasurable and satisfying process, unstringing blackcurrants and seething strawberries, writing the labels recording the jam's fruit and birth date, and at last surveying your platoon of jam-filled jars, the fruits of your labour, lined up on a dark shelf.

BEFORE

Arm yourself with: a 9-litre or 9-quart preserving pan in flavourless thick-based stainless steel (aluminium, brass or copper would also be suitable); a long-handled wooden spoon (hot jam is painful when splashed on the fingers); and a jam funnel (or heat-proof jug). No other special equipment is required.

Rub the base of the preserving pan with butter, which prevents sticking and reduces scum.

Weigh or measure the sugar specified by the recipe and set it to warm in a very low oven.

Wash, rinse and dry a number of 450 g (1 lb) and 900 g (2 lb) glass jars; invert and set them to warm on a large baking sheet in the plate-heating part of the oven or a very slow oven.

Put three small plates in the refrigerator.

Make sure your fruit is perfectly dry, un-bruised, and slightly underripe. Prepare it according to its kind: hull strawberries but do not wash them; unstring blackcurrants from their stems by pulling them through the tines of a fork; leave raspberries alone.

DURING

1. Soften the fruit and release its pectin (the natural gelling agent) by simmering it gently in the preserving pan. Add lemon juice or water at this point if the recipe contains it.

2. Remove from the heat and stir in the warmed sugar with a long-handled spoon. Be patient and wait until it dissolves, or your jam will contain gritty crystals. To test whether it has dissolved, minutely examine the contents of a wooden spoon which you have dipped into the mixture; you should not be able to see any trace of sugar crystals.

3. Boil the jam as fast as you can. The mixture will foam and rise in protest. After a short while the foaming will subside and scum form at the edges; this is the time to test.

4. Test for set; if the jam has boiled long enough, it will set in the required manner when cooled in glass jars. First remove the pan from the heat, then try one of these test methods:

(a) Spoon some jam onto a cold plate taken from the refrigerator. Leave it for a few moments, then nudge it with the side of your finger. If a skin has formed which wrinkles when you prod the jam, then it is ready.

(b) Mix a teaspoon of the mixture with three teaspoonfuls of methylated spirits. Leave for a minute. If it forms one or two large blobs, then the jam is ready. If it breaks into more than three blobs, return the pan to the boil.

(c) Dip a wooden spoon into the mixture, then turn it to cool in the air; if large solidifying flakes form, the jam is ready.

Continue to test at five minute intervals until set point is reached.

AFTERWARDS

Allow the jam to cool for ten minutes, then stir it. This prevents fruit from congregating at the top of the jars.

Using a jam funnel or jug, pour jam into each of the prepared jars until 5 mm ($\frac{1}{4}$ inch) from the rim (the jam will shrink slightly as it grows cold).

Wipe the sides and rims of the jars with a hot damp cloth until splash-free. Place a waxed disc waxed side down over the surface of the jam; press it gently so no air bubbles lurk. Cover with cellophane circles moistened on the outside, held tautly in place by rubber bands. Alternatively, seal the jam's surface by pouring over a little liquid paraffin and allowing it to set in a thin film.

When the jam is quite cold, stick on identifying hand-written labels with the jam's name and the date.

Store in a cool, dry dark place.

P.S. If things go wrong and your jam stays relentlessly runny after it has cooled, tip it all back into the preserving pan and boil, again adding the juice of a lemon, until the right setting point is reached.

STRAWBERRY JAM

——METRIC/IMPERIAL—— •	——CUP MEASURES——
1.8 kg/4 lb strawberries	4 lb strawberries
1.6 kg/3½ lb granulated or preserving sugar	3½ lb sugar
juice of 4 lemons	juice of 4 lemons

Makes about 2.7 kg/6 lb

Choose the smaller fruits, particularly towards the end of the strawberry season when they ripen less well. Ideally, include a few fruits with a little green still on them. Strawberry jam is prettier if the fruits stay whole, for which follow this method: layer the fruits with the sugar in the preserving pan and leave for 24 hours. Add the lemon juice and bring *slowly* to the boil. Stir with great care and gentleness. Boil rapidly for half an hour or just under. When the jam is ready, the strawberries will sink and scum will rise, but carry out your various tests for set anyway.

RASPBERRY JAM

——METRIC/IMPERIAL—— •	——CUP MEASURES——
1.8 kg/4 lb raspberries	4 lb raspberries
1.6 kg/3½ lb granulated or preserving sugar	3½ lb sugar
juice of 4 lemons	juice of 4 lemons

Makes about 2.7 kg/6 lb

Choose very dry fruit, as under-ripe as you can find it. Proceed in the way described for the basic method, crushing a few fruits at the base of the pan to start the juice running. The raspberries will only need to be simmered for 5 minutes; when you add the sugar, keep the pan over a very low heat in order to dissolve it. Boil for about 10 minutes, and it should be ready.

DAMSON JAM

——METRIC/IMPERIAL—— •	——CUP MEASURES——
2.3 kg/5 lb damsons	5 lb damsons
2.7 kg/6 lb granulated or preserving sugar	6 lb sugar
900 ml/1½ pints water	4¼ cups water

Makes about 4.5 kg/10 lb

This is a sharp-flavoured foolproof jam with good setting properties. When you add the sugar, a multitude of damson stones will rise to the surface; remove all of them with a slotted spoon. You will probably have to simmer the fruit for some 35 minutes before it is tender; and boil it for another 10–15 minutes.

BLACKBERRY JAM

——METRIC/IMPERIAL—— •	——CUP MEASURES——
900 g/2 lb blackberries	2 lb blackberries
900 g/2 lb granulated or preserving sugar	4 cups sugar

Makes about 1.4 kg/3 lb

One of the last preserves of summer, this is made from the beautiful dark fruit which grows wild on brambles in late August and September. Early blackberries achieve a more reliable set.

Proceed as for the basic method, simmering for 30 minutes and, after adding the sugar, boiling for 10 minutes.

ROSE PETAL JAM

This surprising jam has a power and delicacy of flavour which goes well with wafer-thin white bread spread with unsalted butter.

——METRIC/IMPERIAL—— •	——CUP MEASURES——
225 g/8 oz dark red rose petals	½ lb dark red rose petals
450 g/1 lb granulated or preserving sugar	1 lb sugar
1.1 litres/2 pints water (clean rainwater if possible)	5 cups water (clean rainwater if possible)
juice of 2 lemons	juice of 2 lemons

Makes about 500 g/1 lb

Snip the white triangles from the rose petal bases, then tear the petals to shreds. Sprinkle them with enough sugar from the main quantity to cover them, and leave overnight. This intensifies the fragrance and darkens the crimson of the petals. Dissolve the sugar in the water and lemon juice over a low heat. Stir in the sugared rose petals and simmer for 20 minutes. Bring to the boil, and boil for 5 minutes until the mixture thickens. This jam is not brought to setting point, so disregard the usual tests. Pot, cover and store in the conventional manner.

LEMON CURD

This is not a jam, of course, but even so it is a summer-flavoured preserve. Its delicious sharpness means that it is very much to modern tastes, while its soft thick texture and yellow opacity go well with brown bread-and-butter. It also makes an unusual filling for a Victoria Sandwich cake.

——METRIC/IMPERIAL—— •	——CUP MEASURES——
grated rind and juice of 2 lemons	grated rind and juice of 2 lemons
1 egg (size 3)	1 medium egg
40 g/1½ oz butter	3 tbsp butter
50 g/2 oz caster sugar	¼ cup superfine sugar

Makes about 225 g/½ lb

Beat the rind, juice and egg together in a heat-proof bowl. Cream the butter and sugar, and stir in to the lemon-scented mixture. Stand the basin over a pan of hot water; stir and beat occasionally until it thickens to bulky creaminess. Pour into a jar, and cover.

SCONES

Scones are very simple, austere little cakes, perfect vehicles for jam and cream. Like shortbread, they provoke competition among cooks; a dozen people can use the same recipe and produce a dozen different batches of scones. Many swear by the efficacy of using sour milk or buttermilk instead of fresh.

METRIC/IMPERIAL	CUP MEASURES
225 g/8 oz self raising flour plus extra for dusting	1½ cups self-rising flour plus extra for dusting
5 ml/1 tsp cream of tartar	1 tsp cream of tartar
2.5 ml/½ tsp bicarbonate of soda	½ tsp baking soda
2.5 ml/½ tsp salt	½ tsp salt
40–50 g/1½–2 oz butter (or lard)	3–4 tbsp butter or shortening
150 ml/¼ pint milk	⅔ cup milk

Oven: 425°F/220°C/Mark 7
Makes about 12 scones

Lightly butter a baking sheet. Sift the flour, cream of tartar, bicarbonate of soda or baking soda and salt into a bowl together. Rub or cut in the butter, fingertipping the mixture into large flakey crumbs. Stir to a soft dough by mixing in the milk with a knife. Roll out to a thickness of 1 cm (½ inch) or just over, and cut into rounds with a pastry-cutter 5–6.5 cm (2–2½ inches) in diameter. Arrange them on the baking sheet fairly close together. Powder their faces with flour. Bake for 12–15 minutes. They will rise and turn golden. They can be served cold, but are excellent while still hot.

STRAWBERRY SHORTCAKE

This cake, splitting scarlet at its seams with strawberries, has the butterfly's lifespan of a single summer's day. It does not keep well; but this is no matter as its invariable cluster of admirers always polish it off within the hour. Another attractive quality is that it is easy and quick to make.

METRIC/IMPERIAL	CUP MEASURES
350 g/12 oz plain flour	3 cups unbleached flour
45 ml/3 tbsp caster sugar	3 tbsp sugar
5 ml/1 tsp salt	1 tsp salt
20 ml/4 tsp baking powder	3 tsp baking powder
250 g/9 oz butter	½ lb (2 sticks) butter
225 ml/⅓ pint double cream	1 cup heavy cream
700 g/1½ lb strawberries	1½ lb strawberries
caster sugar, to taste	sugar, to taste

Oven: 425°F/220°C/Mark 7
Two 20–23 cm (8–9 inch) sandwich or layer cake tins
Makes one shortcake

Butter the sandwich tins. Sift the flour, sugar, salt and baking powder into a large bowl together. Reserve 75 g/3 oz/6 tbsp (¾ stick) of the butter, then rub in or cut in the rest of it to the flour, just as though you were making pastry. Whip the cream to soft peaks, then stir it in with a palette knife or spatula, until you have a pleasant workable dough. Knead for a few seconds only, then divide into two pieces, forming each into a flattened circle. Fit the circles into the prepared tins. Bake for 15–20 minutes.

Turn out the cakes from the tins. Spread one cake with half the remaining butter. Mash about three-quarters of the strawberries with a silver fork, and sweeten them with caster or superfine sugar. Spread them on to the buttered cake. Spread the underneath of the remaining cake with the rest of the butter, and use it to cover the crushed strawberries on top of the first cake. Decorate the top of the whole edifice with the remaining strawberries, left whole. Serve with a jug of whipped cream.

A Directory of Teas

Everyone should build their own hoard of teas. This good habit teaches discernment and educates the palate. Soon you will find yourself moving instinctively to this or that tea to accompany a certain mood or meal. Tea is no mere afternoon beverage, but may be drunk from morning till night without harm. It is a great comfort in life. Dr. Johnson was an early addict who found so, describing himself as a 'hardened and shameless tea-drinker, who has for twenty years diluted his meals with only the infusion of this fascinating plant; whose kettle has scarcely time to cool; who with tea amuses the evening, with tea solaces the midnight, and with tea welcomes the morning.' Tea-drinking is one of those rare pleasures which are both civilised and cost next to nothing. Apart from water, tea is the least expensive drink in the world, even if you buy the very best. Tea-drinking is a cheerful habit to cultivate, as each cup gently shifts fatigue, lifts the spirits and brightens the brainbox. De Quincy, who was pretty much an expert when it came to ways of palliating the harshness of life, wrote that 'tea, though ridiculed by those who are naturally coarse in their nervous sensibilities, or are become so from wine-drinking, and are not susceptible of influence from so refined a stimulant, will always be the favoured beverage of the intellectual.'

THE ESSENTIAL TEA CADDY

'Your Tea-Leaf tho' never so good when you buy, will lose itself, being of a very volatile Spirit, unless carefully preserv'd in Silver, Pewter, or Tin Boxes, shut close from the Air; and above All, kept from the Damps, and Neighbourhood of strong Scents, whether sweet or offensive.'

From A Treatise on the Inherent Qualities of the Tea-Herb, Compiled by a Gentleman of Cambridge 1750

A Good Tea Guide

First sample the classic black teas of India and Ceylon, whose taste is familiar to much of the Western world in the form of popular brand-name blends. Try these teas unblended to appreciate their separate flavours, fragrance and colour in the cup. They are usually taken with a little milk.

ASSAM

Brisk, bracing and strongly-coloured, this is what the British popularly expect from a cup of tea. Known for its malty forthrightness, excellent in winter and foul weather. The boldest of teas.

DARJEELING

Famous as the champagne among teas, light-coloured, with a distinctive bouquet often described as flowery or blackcurranty. A delicate wine-like Muscatel flavour.

NILGIRI

This tea is light and clean and mellow to taste; it pours out a bright brisk liquor.

CEYLON

Grown at the high altitudes which provide the best growing conditions for tea, Ceylon teas are bright, steady, and turn an attractive golden colour when milk is added to the cup. Their number includes teas from Dimbula, Uva and Nuwara Eliya. All Ceylon teas have a fine refreshing flavour.

Now taste a couple of China's fine black teas, quite different from those in our first group, with a history a hundred times more ancient.

KEEMUN

The tea of Imperial China, clean, delicate, with a light fruity sweetness on its breath. Its liquor is pale gold and the Chinese say it has the flavour of an orchid. Drink with or without milk.

LAPSANG SOUCHONG

A bracing large-leafed tea, this is either loved or hated, leaving no room for ambivalence. It tastes of woodsmoke and has a tarry pungency (supposedly owing to the particular soil of the Fujian Province of China where it is grown). It pours out to a clear bright colour like whisky, very cheerful, and smells a little of smoked salmon or grilled bacon. Good open-air tea. Never add milk.

Unfermented green teas from China are quite another beverage from all that have gone before. They are never taken with milk, though some people like to add lemon.

JASMINE

A large-leafed tea, semi-fermented, scented with jasmine flowers (which are generally left in the tea, later to expand beautifully and aromatically in your teapot of boiling water).

GUNPOWDER

One of China's oldest teas, its large greyish-green leaves are rolled into pellets resembling lead shot. You need less tea than usual to make a pot of Gunpowder. Its liquor contradicts its belligerent name, being thin, pale, shy, slightly bitter and straw-coloured. The Chinese call it pearl tea. It has a lower caffeine level than any other tea.

LUNG CHING

Highly esteemed by the Chinese, this tea has a delicate vegetative flavour, ethereal and slightly sweet. Its liquor is a pale emerald colour.

One tea remains on its own, of singular magnificence, more expensive than any of the others, grown on the island of Taiwan (Formosa).

FORMOSA OOLONG

A partially-fermented China tea which holds an exquisite flavour of ripe peaches. Its liquor is the colour of amber. At its best, it is full of leaf tips. Its low caffeine content makes it a good tea to drink before retiring to bed. (There are other Oolong teas from China, but this one is beyond compare.)

The whole business of tea-drinking acquires an additional sophistication with the issue of blending. Monarchs and social lions have often had blends named after them. You can contrive your own mixtures, or choose from the following classic blends.

EARL GREY

Named after the second Earl Grey in 1830, during his spell as Prime Minister under William IV. The story goes that one of the Earl's envoys saved the life of a Mandarin while on a diplomatic mission to China. The Mandarin showed his gratitude by sending Earl Grey a delicately-scented blend of tea. Today, Earl Grey tea is generally made from large-leafed China tea, Darjeeling, and oil of bergamot (which is a pear-shaped Mediterranean citrus fruit). It is wonderfully fragrant, and good with cakes and sweet things.

LADY LONDONDERRY

This lady was a popular society hostess during the first quarter of this century. She had her own blend of Ceylon, Indian and Formosa tea made for her by Jacksons of Piccadilly.

RUSSIAN CARAVAN

Tea used to be carried by camel caravan from China across the mountains and deserts of Asia to Russia. The last such caravan left Peking for Russia in 1900. This blend traditionally holds the finest Keemun teas and may contain some Oolong too.

Even the cheapest brand-name blends of tea hold three basic elements: Indian tea for strength; Ceylon tea for flavour; and African tea (which is rarely sold pure under its own name) for its dark hearty colour. (Cheap neutral teas make up the rest of the blend's bulk, and reduce the price.) Between ten and forty teas are used in each of this sort of blend. Good quality blends of Indian and Ceylon teas are often called Breakfast teas. English Breakfast tea is usually a strong blend of small-leafed Indian and Ceylon teas, full-flavoured and satisfying. Irish breakfast tea is even stronger, comprising a high proportion of Assam with a little fine-flavoured Ceylon, giving a bold rousing cup.

Black China teas blend well together, but outside their own family can only bear introduction to the finest, most delicate Ceylon and Darjeeling teas. A pinch of green tea (particularly Gunpowder) added to a conservative blend of black tea greatly improves the flavour. Oolong teas bring out the characteristics of other teas when you add a very small quantity to the main mixture; try just half a teaspoon of Oolong with the normal amount of Ceylon or Darjeeling to test the truth of this.

Buy loose tea by the chest or half-chest, and split it with friends; the leaves will still have their bloom. Tea stays fresh for months if properly stored.

Keep it in an airtight tin or caddy.

The Tea Leaf:
How to Brew and not to Stew

In the first book about tea, the eighth-century *Ch'a Ching*, its author, Lu Yu, asserted that the ideal tea leaf should 'curl like the dewlaps of a bull, crease like the leather boots of a Tartar horseman, unfold like mist rising over a ravine, and soften as gently as fine earth swept by rain.' Be that as it may, the larger the tea leaf, the longer you should allow it to infuse; the smaller it is, the more quickly its flavour floods from it. The tiniest leaves (called Dust in tea jargon) are used in tea bags and yield almost instant infusion. Allow five to six minutes infusion time for the larger-leafed teas (technically termed Orange Pekoes or Pekoes, names which refer only to the size of the leaves, not to their flavour or quality); but only three minutes for the smaller grades (known as Broken Pekoes and Fannings).

What about the Problem of the Wasted Pot? The first cup is perfect, but while that is being drunk, the rest of the pot stews and is tainted by tannin. To solve this, follow Mrs Beeton's tip and decant one pot to another (make sure both are well warmed), once the infusion time is reached. Or copy Dr. Johnson and pour all the perfectly-brewed tea at once into a two-quart cup. Or use a tea-ball infuser, removing it after the requisite number of minutes. If you make sure that the tea leaves are removed after the right time (by whatever means), you can then safely employ a tea cosy to keep the rest hot, and each cup will be as bright and fresh and steaming as the first.

HOW TO MAKE A PERFECT POT OF TEA

Empty your kettle, then fill it with freshly-drawn water from the cold tap.

Put the kettle on and, just before it comes to the boil, pour a generous dash of the hot water into your teapot (glazed china or earthenware for preference), swirling it round and round inside the pot before pouring it away. (Warming the pot is not a meaningless ritual, but ensures that the water stays at boiling point when it hits the tea, encouraging the proper opening of the leaves.)

Dole out one heaped teaspoon of tea leaves for each person and one for the pot, straight into the warmed teapot. (Large-leafed teas are comparatively light for their volume, so add an extra spoon or so of these.) The kettle will have reached a galloping boil by this time, so pour the water over the tea. Take care that the water is not long boiling; over-boiled water loses its oxygen and results in a bitter muddy brew of tea.

Allow the tea to stand and brew for anything from three to six minutes according to the leaf size (less time for small leaves, more for large ones).

Give the tea a good stir and pour it, using a strainer to catch leaves. If you take your tea with milk, you should add it to the cup, *cold* and fresh, before pouring the tea.

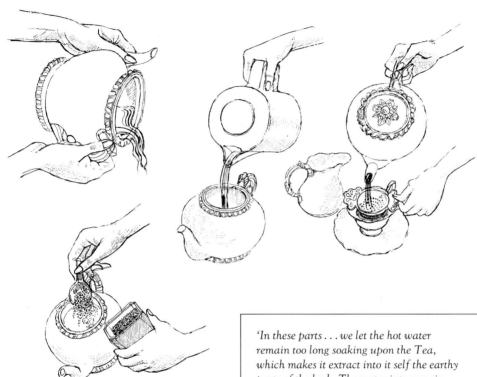

P.S. Tea bags are never a good idea. The tea they produce is simply not the same. Also, try not to add sugar to tea as it vitiates the taste. As Fielding wrote, 'Love and scandal are the best sweeteners of tea.'

'In these parts . . . we let the hot water remain too long soaking upon the Tea, which makes it extract into it self the earthy parts of the herb. The water is to remain upon it, no longer than whiles you can say the Miserere Psalm very leisurely. . . . Thus you have only the spiritual parts of the Tea, which is much more active, penetrating and friendly to nature.'
The Closet of the Eminently Learned Sir Kenelm Digby Knight Opened, 1669

Index

African tea 61
Afternoon tea 15–17, 19
Alice B. Toklas Sandwich 24
Assam tea 20, 59, 61

Black teas 59, 61
Blackberry Jam 55
Blended teas 61
Bohea tea 13
Bone china 16–17
Boston tea-party 13
Brandy Snaps 37
Bread-and-butter 22
Breakfast teas 61
Broken Pekoe teas 62
Brownies 44

Caffeine 23, 60
Cakes 22, 32–51, 57
  at the Ritz 8
  Brandy Snaps 37
  Brownies 44
  Classic Fatless Sponge 36
  Coconut 33
  Devil's Food 45
  Dundee 49
  Eccles 47–48
  Flapjacks 47
  Florentines 43
  Fruit 38–39
  Gingerbread Husbands 50
  Grantham Gingerbreads 51
  Helen's Rich Gingerbread 51
  Macaroons 41–42
  Madeira 33
  Madeleines 40–41
  Marble 35
  Meringues 42
  Panforte 44–45
  Rock 47
  Seed 34
  Shortbread 48
  Strawberry Shortcake 57
  Victoria Sandwich 37
  See also Pastries, Teacakes

Ceylon tea 59, 61
Children's teas 22–23
China tea 13, 59–61
Chocolate Eclairs 10
Cinnamon Toast 27
Classic Fatless Sponge Cake 36
Club Man's tea 20–21
Coconut Cake 33
Creamware, see Queensware
Crumpets 28
Cucumber Sandwich 19

Damson Jam 55
Darjeeling tea 59, 61
Devilled Ham Toasts 22
Devil's Food Cake 45
Drop Scones 31
Dundee Cake 49

Earl Grey tea 60
Eccles Cakes 47–48
English Breakfast tea 61
English Muffins 29
English Rabbit 21

Fannings 62
Flapjacks 47
Florentines 43
Formosa Oolong tea 60
Fruit Cake 38–39

Gentleman's Club tea 20–21
Gentleman's Relish 20
Gingerbread Husbands 50
Gingerbreads 50–51
Grantham Gingerbreads 51
Green teas 59, 61
Gunpowder tea 59–60, 61

Helen's Rich Gingerbread 51
High tea 46–47
Hyson tea 13

Indian tea 14–15, 59, 61
Irish Breakfast tea 61

Jam-making 53–56
Jams 55–56
Jasmine tea 59

Keemun tea 59, 61
Kettle 62

Lady Londonderry tea 61

Lapsang Souchong tea 59
Lemon Curd 56
Lung Ching tea 60

Macaroons 41–42
Madeira Cake 33
Madeleines 40–41
Marble Cake 35
Mayonnaise for egg sandwiches 20
Meringues 42
Mille Feuilles 8–9
Minton china 15
Muffins 28–29

Nilgiri tea 59
Nursery tea 22–23

Oolong teas 60, 61
Orange Pekoe teas 62

Panforte 44–45
Pastries 8–11
  at the Ritz 8
  Chocolate Eclairs 10
  Mille Feuilles 8–9
  Puff Pastry 9–10
  Strawberry Tarts 11
Patum Peperium, see Gentleman's Relish
Pekoe teas 62
Pitta Pockets Zazou 25
Plum cake, see Fruit Cake
Porcelain 13, 14, 16–17
  Derby 13
  Worcester 13
Potted Shrimps 20–21
Pre-theatre tea 23
Puff Pastry 9–10

Queensware 14

Raspberry Jam 55
Ritz, César 6
Ritz's Special Egg Sandwiches 20
Ritz's Special Smoked Salmon Sandwiches 25
Rock Cakes 47
Rose Petal Jam 56
Russian caravan tea 61

Sandwich, Earl of 18
Sandwiches 18
  Alice B. Toklas 24
  banana 23
  children's 22–23
  Club Man's 20
  cucumber 19

peanut-butter-and-jelly 23
Ritz's Special Egg 20
Ritz's Special Smoked Salmon 25
sardine 23
striped 25
tomato 23
watercress 24
York ham and mustard 20
Savoury tea dishes 21
Scones 8, 56–57
Scotch Woodcock 21
Scrambled Egg with Smoked Salmon 24
Seed Cake 34
Shortbread 48
Spode, Josiah 16–17
Sponge cakes 36–37
Stewed tea 62
Strawberry Shortcake 57
Strawberry Tarts 11
Sugar in tea 63

Tannin 62
Tea 59–61
  Ceylon 59, 61
  China 13, 59–61
  Indian 14–15, 61
Tea bags 62, 63
Tea caddy 58
Tea Cakes 30
Tea clippers 15
Tea infuser 62
Tea leaves, size of 62
Tea services 12–13, 16
Tea urns 17
Tea-drinking 58, 60
  history of 12–17, 19
Tea-making 62–63
Tea-parties 37
Teapots 12, 13, 15, 17
Teashops 17
Toast 27
Toasting fork 26, 27
Tomato Sandwiches 23
Twankey tea 13

Unblended teas 59–60

Victoria Sandwich 37

Warming the teapot 62
Watercress Sandwich 24
Wedgwood, Thomas 14
Welsh Rarebit 23

Yeast 30